THE **SMART CONSUMER'S**

Book of Questions

LINDA MACK ROSS

CHICAGO
REVIEW
PRESS

Library of Congress Cataloging-in-Publication Data

Ross, Linda Mack.
    The smart consumer's book of questions / by Linda Mack Ross. —
1st ed.
       p.   cm.
    ISBN 1-55652-265-7
    1. Consumer education.   I. Title.
TX335.R692 1996
640'.73—dc20
                                                              96-3241
                                                                  CIP

Published by Chicago Review Press, Incorporated
814 North Franklin Street
Chicago, Illinois 60610
ISBN 1-55652-265-7
Printed in the United States of America
5 4 3 2 1

In fond memory of my parents, Hilda and Irving Mack, who usually responded to my incessant questioning with, "What are you writing, a book?" Could it be more appropriate?

In loving appreciation to my children, Jonah and Hillary, who continually question my questions and are still learning that they don't have all the answers.

Contents

Preface

My intention in writing this book was twofold. Years of listening to people describe their bad consumer experiences — often the same experiences, and often ones I have had myself — convinced me that we have these experiences because we don't know what questions to ask of service providers, suppliers, organizations, and salespeople before we make our decisions. I wanted to share successes and failures so that consumers could learn from each other and minimize their own mistakes. I also wanted to find a way to make lemonade out of lemons, to turn some of my negative experiences into positives, at least for others.

What I didn't anticipate was the money I have saved because of what I learned in researching and writing this book. I now spend four hundred dollars less per year on my insurance than I used to. By negotiating with my long-distance company, I received some free long-distance calling privileges during specified times. I found a long-distance service for my credit card calls that waives the eighty-cent surcharge that major long-distance companies currently require. I continue to reap the benefits of this. I have found a better banking deal, learned more about financial planners and planning, and have gotten better at negotiating because of this book.

Family, friends, and acquaintances have also benefited from my research and are saving money because they are making more informed decisions. This book is especially useful for parents to give to older children who may need advice but prefer not to hear it from mom or dad.

Use this book as you embark on a new consumer adventure — undergoing a life transition, making a major purchase, hiring a specialist, reassessing a previous decision — to get the best deals and the service you deserve. Join me in receiving the benefits of asking the right questions.

Acknowledgments

This book was created directly and indirectly by many people. I am eternally grateful to the countless people who have contributed to this book by responding to questionnaires, communicating through CompuServe forums, answering specific questions, sharing their stories, and inviting me into their various organizations as a consultant. At this point, I am even thankful to those people who pushed me to the point of aggravation that motivated me to write this book. I can't name everyone, but many of the contributors and antagonists know who they are.

Al Honrath brainstormed this book with me and helped with the initial survey.

There were those who took time to provide in-depth help about topics they were familiar with: Ruth Goldberg, Rhoda Levin, Steven Heller, Elliot Pinck, Gary Bloom, Barbara Putnam, Carol Woodard, Janet Weivoda, Sandy Goodman, Judy Cofman, Chuck Cook, Carrie Oleisky, Elaine Woldorsky, Allan Seely, Jim Larson, Jim Stathopoulos, Arthur Wiss, Jonah Ross, Hillary Ross, Sandy Larson, Sue Mahmoodi, Margaret Telfer and other librarians at Hill Library, Vicki Palmquist, Joyce Orbuch, Shelly

Kordell, Serene Abrahams, Nancy Welsh, Katheryn Lundquist, Jay Dworsky, Art Mack, and Doug Menikheim.

Sharon Gelperin, Harriet Wiss, Yolanda Maya, Marilyn Furmansky, and Raleigh Rigler took the time to read and contribute to many chapters of this book. Jeannie Hanson, my agent, provided encouragement, help, and enthusiasm.

There were those who contributed to this book in more subtle ways: David Wark, Jerry Allan, Noel Larson, Ruth Bly, Bea Pieper, Anne Moen, and Barb Garland helped me uncover answers and see possibilities; Ivan Ross opened doors for me; Marcy Gust kept me organized, shared her wisdom, and was there for me; Bill and Sue Markham showed me creativity and perseverance and provided me with many enriching experiences; Rick Passon supported me and kept my mind busy with questions I hadn't thought of; and The Bush Foundation granted me a fellowship to study Alternative Dispute Resolution.

Introduction

It is better to know some of the questions than all of the answers.
　　　　　　　　　　　　　　　　　　—James Thurber

How often have you or someone you know had a negative consumer experience? How much energy, time, and money have been spent because of these bad experiences? How much aggravation and stress have you experienced trying to correct injustices and reverse bad consumer decisions? Much more than you would have liked, I'm sure.

After countless bad experiences, the light bulb finally went on for me in 1987 when I bought my house.

The day before the sale was to close, the city condemned my deck. A city inspector told me to replace the deck with treated lumber, which I did. Several months later a "stop-building" sign appeared on my deck. Since I wasn't building anything I pulled the sign off. Within days an irate building inspector stood at my door shouting that I had violated a city building code. I could barely understand him and asked for clarification. He said I needed a building permit to build a deck.

"I didn't build a deck," I replied. "I followed the city inspector's instructions and replaced it with treated lumber." It turned out that replacing meant building and I needed a permit.

"How was I to know?" I asked. "I was just following instructions."

"That's ridiculous," he replied. "It's like saying you shouldn't get a ticket for going seventy on a street where thirty is the speed limit."

"Not at all," I said. "I had to pass a test to drive, and learn the rules. How would I know all the laws governing my home? Why didn't the inspector tell me that replacing the deck would require a building permit?"

"Well, why didn't you ask?" he said.

That's when it hit me. I hadn't asked because I didn't think to do so.

So often we don't know what questions to ask when we're making purchases or hiring service providers. They, in turn, don't realize what we don't know. And so, even with the best of intentions, the situation becomes complicated and expensive. Knowing the questions to ask can save time, money, and aggravation.

My experience with my deck is not uncommon. A similar miscommunication was related to me recently: Sandy and Roger sold their townhouse to move out of state. They were relieved to sell the townhouse and thrilled to get the price they asked. As they were negotiating the sale, they told the buyers, Jennifer and Michael, to get a booklet about the development's rules and regulations from the management company.

Jennifer and Michael were excited about buying their first home. It was their dream home in a perfect location. As the closing grew near, Jennifer mentioned something to Sandy about her dog. Sandy said she didn't know that Jennifer had a dog and asked if Jennifer knew the complex prohibited pets.

Jennifer did not know. As much as Jennifer and Michael loved their new home, they were not willing to give up the dog and wanted to break their contract. Sandy and Roger were all ready to move, and they were not willing to break the contract. Everyone was angry and frustrated.

In this situation there was no intention to mislead anyone. Should the owners have mentioned that the complex did not allow pets? Should the buyers have asked? The buyers didn't *know* to ask. They assumed they could have an animal in their own home. The sellers, accustomed to the many rules of the complex, didn't think of going over each and every rule.

Why Do We Need to Ask Questions?

In his article "Suggestions for Choosing a Professional Planner" in *Nation's Business*, April 1993, Peter Weaver quoted Patti Houlihan, a Virginia-based financial planner and former host of the Public Broadcasting Service television series "The Financial Adviser." When asked the biggest mistake people make when interviewing a prospective financial planner, Houlihan answered, "Not having the nerve to ask tough questions."

Even if some of us are experts in certain areas, we can't know enough about everything we need to know, do, and have in our lives. Information, technology, and procedures change so rapidly, we often make decisions without knowing and understanding all of our options. It becomes more important to know how to get information than it is to know a perhaps outdated answer.

It is also crucial to know the accuracy of the information you receive. In my work as a market research project manager I encountered interviewers who falsified research. Subsequent statistics, information, and decisions may be based on this inaccurate, invalid, and unreliable data. Asking for clarification will help you understand the significance of information.

We need to ask questions to take care of ourselves, to increase knowledge and awareness, to decrease negative experiences, and ultimately to make the best decisions. The most valuable question of all may be: Is there anything I need to know that I didn't ask?

What Can This Book Do for You?

While I was working on this book, my son graduated from college and moved to California. As he left he asked, "Is your chapter on renting apartments finished? I don't know what to ask." I was shocked when I realized that I, who am so big on asking questions, had not thought about coaching him in the process of choosing an apartment and signing a lease.

That made me realize that sometimes we don't think about information others may need to know. This book proved to be even handier than I realized. Had I simply *told* my son what he needed to know, I have little faith that I would have covered all the bases or he would have remembered all my advice. Instead he was able to take the apartment chapter as a checklist, think about what he needed to look for as he walked through apartments, and then ask the questions that were important to him.

This book provides the questions to ask and the process to follow so you can make the best choices. It's quick: you don't have to bog yourself down with details, just become better informed about what you need. You will have an easily accessible guide and a checklist to follow to assist you as various situations arise.

Since every community has different regulations, policies, and laws, asking the questions can help you determine what applies for where you live. For example, the teacher-student ratio at child-care facilities may differ from state to state and from urban to rural areas. Building codes often differ from suburb to suburb within the same metropolitan area. Services provided by each library are different, community to community. Licensure renewals for professionals vary. Family laws, interpretations, and practices that influence child custody, divorce proceedings, and alimony can differ from county to county. Asking questions is crucial because so many of the products and services we seek are subject to constant change.

This book is comprehensive. The questions come from people who have suffered losses as a result of bad consumer experiences and who have learned how to be more successful. Professionals from various fields also contributed insider information, insights, and experiences. The book is a tool; it draws upon others' successes and failures to help future consumers. Some people, particularly our children, often don't want advice. They want to find their own way. This book can help people see their choices in an objective way. They can select the issues that are important to them.

What Is the Best Way to Use This Book?

For a crash course in consumer savvy about a wide variety of topics, you can read from page one to the end, or you can use this book one chapter at a time, as different choices come up in your life. In addition to the list of questions, each chapter tells a true story about how I or someone else fared when making choices similar to yours. Other people's mistakes can thus be put to good use.

Read the appropriate chapter and decide which questions are most important to you. Some of the questions you may want to answer through research before going to the store or attending a meeting. Ideally people you meet with will provide you with much of the information you need without you having to ask all the questions. Rather than immediately asking and checking off questions, see what information you receive. Or ask a general question like *Tell me about this product, service, or process and about your background.*

After hearing from the salesperson or service provider, assess which questions haven't been answered. Ask your most important questions first. Your questions may be more warmly received if you use this book as a checklist. Explain that as a consumer you want to make sure you understand the process and have realistic expectations.

The questions in this book are helpful not just as you embark on a new purchase of goods or services; they also enable you to evaluate choices you've made. I have greatly benefited by researching this book. There were so many questions I didn't know to ask when I bought services and products. The questions inspired me to learn more about services I was already receiving. I have now changed some of my service providers, saved money, and feel happier and more content with what I have.

You may find that just seeing a question is the key you have been looking for, one that opens a door for you.

How Can Service Providers and Businesses Benefit from This Book?

By using this book as a checklist, business owners and service providers will ensure that customers are provided with the information they need to make smart choices. Most businesses get their customers by referrals and know that satisfied customers are crucial. According to the Direct Selling Education Foundation, a customer who has an unpleasant shopping experience shares this with an average of nine or ten other people. It is likely that each of these people will, in turn, tell others about this negative experience. Therefore, significant damage to a business' reputation can occur as the result of one bad customer experience.

In the *Popcorn Report* published in 1992, Faith Popcorn wrote about the growth of the Vigilante Consumer. Evolved from the protest generation, today's consumers research, investigate, question, challenge, and protest. According to the report there are more than two hundred consumer boycott groups. As she states, no one likes to be fooled or ignored.

Happy, empowered customers are a benefit to you. They will be loyal customers if you provide them with the answers and the respect they need to make the best choices for themselves.

Your Questions Are Important Because:

Some people are better at what they do than others. Not all salespeople or service providers are equally knowledgeable or skilled. Asking questions will help you decide whether the person you are working with has the expertise you need. What are the training, education, and experience of the people you plan to hire or buy from? Will they provide references to vouch for the quality of their work? How long have they been in business? How much product knowledge do they have? Can they compare products? What kind of warranties do they offer? How much time are they willing to spend with you to make sure you understand the product or service?

Most people are in business to make money. Some are shortsighted and don't realize you are a potential "salesperson." Be aware of whose pocketbook they are watching out for. They may try to sell you more than what you want or need.

If people are focused on getting your business or selling you a product, they will tell you what they think you want to hear. Ask questions in different ways to assure you are really getting what is best for you.

Questions bridge understanding. Asking questions gives people opportunities to understand another person's perspective.

Information and technology change daily. You may not know everything about the latest developments in the product or service under consideration, but professionals you are working with should. Do they keep current? What are the advances in the field? Is what you are purchasing up-to-date? Is the best technology being used? How quickly will the product be outdated? Is there a trade-in option and value?

All humans make mistakes. Ask the questions you need to make sure things are happening as you expected and that you are receiving what you purchased. Protect yourself so that someone else's mistake does not cost you time and money. (And be forgiving so it doesn't cost you your health.)

We all make assumptions. Clarify, clarify, clarify . . . every little thing. Procedures keep changing and our expectations may be based on old ways. People have different interpretations of words and events. Be specific.

You are the customer and can control whom you hire and whom you retain. Many years ago a friend of mine fired her mother's doctor because he wasn't sharing information about her mother's health with her family and treated my friend condescendingly. The dismissal was shocking at the time. But now, since more people are taking charge of their lives, it is a more common occurrence.

You are most important to yourself. To a professional you are one of many, a small part of a case load or customer base. Cancer may be routine for a doctor but not for the patient. You deserve to be treated as an important, unique individual.

You win some, you lose some. Even if we do all we can, things may not turn out the way we want; it is the pattern of life. You want to maximize your chances of winning. Even if you don't, you might have recourse to correct a mistake, get reimbursed, or obtain new services or equipment. Try to acknowledge and express your anger, get your needs met, learn from mistakes, and move on.

What If I Am Not Comfortable Asking Questions?

We have all been programmed with messages and rules throughout our lives. Our programming comes from our families, schools, friends, religious institutions, the media, history, peers, workplaces, and from our own experiences, often from our childhood. Old messages, insecurities, and assumptions can be barriers to asking questions, to taking care of ourselves. To maximize our interactions we need to understand ourselves and how we may be standing in our own way.

While we all have different experiences, messages, and rules, there are many similarities. Sometimes we may fear the outcome of asking a question. Will people think I am stupid? Will they not accept me? One editor who reviewed my book thought if she asked too many questions as she looked at summer camps for her child they might think she was weird and wouldn't want her child or would treat her child differently. Asking questions is taking a risk. Since my child incurred injuries at a camp that didn't train counselors and campers about emergency procedures, my first concern is safety. I believe it is better to risk offending the camp than risk my child's life. Better we take care of ourselves than worry what others think.

Our ability to ask questions may be affected by some of the old messages and rules we learned such as these: Children should be seen and not heard (there are adults who haven't changed their behavior based on that message). Assertiveness is sometimes interpreted as aggressiveness, which is often viewed negatively. Some people may think it is demanding to ask questions or that asking questions may be intrusive, disrespectful, or impolite, especially when questioning elders.

Often old messages are responsible for our assumptions. We may not feel deserving or believe that we are entitled to get the best. We may assume people in charge have our best interest at heart when they don't. We or they may have a strong need to be right or look like an expert and lose objectivity. Many of us are uncomfortable with anger, conflict, and disagreement. "Peace at any price" can result in internal warfare.

Sometimes questions are used to avoid being direct. We say, *How would you like to take out the garbage?* We really mean, I would like the garbage to be taken out; would you mind doing it? We do much better at taking care of ourselves when we ask direct questions and not expect others to read our minds.

As consumers, we need to be able to get our needs met. We need to ask for what we want even when we may have been told no. I have been to several restaurants where waiters indicated that what I wanted wasn't available. However, when I requested that they ask, the chef was more than happy to prepare the dish for me.

If you are uncomfortable asking questions, it may show, and you won't get the answers. When I managed market research projects I could tell which interviewers weren't comfortable asking certain demographic questions because they consistently didn't get the answers. Since I am quite comfortable asking the questions, I usually get the answers.

Get in touch with your own discomfort about asking questions, try to identify the source, and realize that to take care of yourself you need to ask questions. Watch your negative feelings when you ask questions and learn to manage them with positive self-talk. You have the right to take care of yourself.

The people you hire or contract with are also programmed with old messages. They may assume you know more than you do. Asking questions can trigger their insecurities; they may feel threatened. They may think questions challenge their professionalism or credibility. They may think you don't trust them. They may resent having questions asked.

What Is the Best Way to Ask Questions?

How you ask and phrase questions, the tone you use, and your body language can influence the responses you get. People may become defensive or may not understand what you are trying to find out. An explanation of what you want to accomplish and a question asking for help or clarification will get you off to a useful start.

There are standard questions to ask and processes to follow with most interactions. Trust your gut. If things don't seem right to you, follow your intuition. Try to discover the priorities of those you'll be working with, their education and experience, how they handle mishaps, and whether they will assist you if things do go wrong. The best source is a referral, people you know who are happy with the service or product they paid for. But remember to determine the priorities of the people making referrals so you know if they have the same standards and expectations you have.

All of us make mistakes. It is important to know how people handle mistakes and rectify errors. Ask those you are seeking to hire or buy from about errors they have made and how they have solved problems. If they don't admit to making errors, think twice about doing business with them. Other red flags: people who avoid answering key questions, resent your questions, and treat you abruptly and disrespectfully.

We can help others understand our situation better by identifying similar situations in their own lives. For example, I have talked to technical people who didn't understand my need for information. By asking them to recall their own experiences, perhaps with a doctor, where they felt uninformed or inadequate, I brought them closer to my concerns.

My experience is that many people want to be helpful. Some questions may seem too private, but you will be surprised what people will tell if you ask in a caring, respectful way and listen attentively.

Questions That Apply to Every Situation

There are many questions we can ask ourselves as we go through life that will help us make better decisions. These questions apply in most situations:

❑ What are my objectives? What do I really want?

❑ Have I identified all my options?

❑ Have I gotten all the information I need?

❑ What assumptions am I making that I need to clarify?

❑ How does my gut feel about this? How much is enough— how much do I need?

❑ Am I doing this for others or for myself?

❑ Is this decision in my best interest for both the short and long run? What do I have to lose?

❑ If people close to me don't like my decision, what am I going to say to them and to myself?

❑ Is this worth my time, energy, money, and the hassle?

❑ What kind of help or support might I need?

❑ Am I expressing myself as clearly as I can? Are my actions congruent with my words?

❑ Do I have unrealistic expectations of myself? Of others? What do others expect of me?

❑ Are other people thinking of me or taking care of themselves?

❑ How do I know I am accomplishing what I want to accomplish?

❑ Is this a win-win situation?

❑ If this is such a good deal, why isn't everyone doing it?

PART ONE

On the Road

Making
Travel Plans

Many years ago when vacationing in Israel, we stopped at the American Express office to reconfirm our flight out the next day. "Your reservations were canceled," we were told. You had to reconfirm three days before your flight. The only way we could keep to our itinerary was to buy first-class seats to London—a very costly option. *Lessons learned:* Read the fine print on your tickets. Ask your agent about confirmations or any other travel tips you may need for different countries.

When you make travel plans it is most important to know yourself. Also remember that your mood at the time may influence your choice. If you feel tired you may choose a restful vacation and be sorry you are not busier when the time comes. You may think that you want to vacation with a friend or partner but crave time alone when the vacation arrives. To maximize your travel experiences, try to make plans that will allow you to do all you like. Set boundaries and be clear with traveling partners about your needs and desires. You may need to negotiate, but be sure to take care of yourself.

There is a big difference in travel agents. Some look for cheaper fares, others might provide more comprehensive services. Everybody comes from a different perspective. If you use a travel agent or listen to a friend's travel advice, try to understand their priorities. For example, if your travel agent is more concerned about bargains, she may recommend something that is not as appealing to you if your priorities have to do with ambiance or amenities.

Ask Yourself

❑ Has the agent been recommended by people who have similar likes and dislikes or similar values?

❑ Have I checked fares with the airlines or other agents to ensure I'm getting the best price?

❑ Do I trust my travel agent?

❑ What are my priorities regarding this vacation? Do I want a vacation that is busy, restful, active, educational, or a combination?

❑ Do I have the time and energy to plan a demanding itinerary, or do I need to keep things simple?

❑ Do I want to spend time by myself? With family or friends? Meet new people?

❑ Do I want to be able to spend time with and get to know local people?

❑ Do I want to see new sites or scenery?

❑ Do I want an overview of a region or do I want an in-depth experience of a smaller area?

❑ What kinds of facilities do I prefer: swimming pool, tennis courts, cable TV, kitchen, children's activities, and so forth?

❑ What kind of entertainment do I want to attend?

❑ What kind of activities do I want to participate in?

❑ Do I want to go to my destination immediately or do I want to enjoy getting there?

❑ Will there be enough to do if I decide I want more activity?

❑ How much money am I willing to spend?

❑ Do I want to dress casually, formally, or both?

❑ How much time am I willing to spend to get to the activities or destinations I want to include on my vacation?

❑ What is the best travel guide to meet my needs?

Preplanning

Ask Traveling Companions

❑ What do you want and need?

❑ What kinds of lodging and restaurants do you prefer?

❑ Are you willing to negotiate on planning the trip? Making changes after we arrive?

❑ How important is cost to you? What if trip expenses exceed our estimate?

❑ If we need to negotiate, what are your priorities? What are you willing to give up?

❑ If things don't work out the way we plan, how do you adjust to change and disappointment?

❑ What are your sleeping habits or needs?

Ask a Travel Agent

❑ Do you look for the lowest fare?

❑ If a cheaper fare becomes available after I book the ticket, can I get money back for the difference? Will you be aware of those fares and automatically reimburse me? How far in advance do I need to purchase a ticket to get the best fare?

❑ Do you check with consolidators?

❑ Do you deliver tickets?

❑ Have you been to the destination you are recommending? To the hotel?

❑ What kind of experiences have other clients had with this tour or trip?

Selecting a Method of Travel

❑ What transportation (boat, train, plane) would best meet my needs?

❑ Are there specific physical or psychological needs of co-travelers that will be better served by a specific mode of transportation?

❑ What are the time, money, and weather constraints that influence my choice of transportation?

❑ Am I getting the best travel rate? Would it be cheaper to fly into one country and out of another? Is there something about the season, holidays, or special events that make it more expensive to fly into this country at this time?

❑ Are certain modes of transportation (bus, train, plane) offering special fares during my vacation period?

❑ Are there certain times (days and hours) I can travel cheaper?

❑ Do I want to see scenery or explore on the way to my destination? If so, what time of day will provide me with the best views?

❑ Do I want to maximize time and perhaps money by traveling while I am sleeping?

❑ Is food provided? Is there a place to purchase full meals or snacks? What is the price range?

❑ Are there smoking and nonsmoking sections?

❑ How flexible are the travel arrangements ? If I need to, can I change plans? Will there be a penalty? How much of a penalty?

❑ Are there any passes I can buy such as a Eurail pass that will give me flexibility but still be economical?

Selecting Destinations

❑ What are the variations in weather this time of year?

❑ Will the weather conditions allow me to do what I want in this area?

❑ Are there special events taking place at the destination that could affect my plans—make it more enjoyable, crowded, more expensive, more difficult to get hotel rooms, car rentals and restaurant reservations?

❑ Can I be flexible and forgo reservations?

Selecting a Tour

❑ Are the tour arrangers specialists in the location I want to go to or in the activities that interest me?

❑ Are there specific tours that address my special interests?

❑ Have I looked into learning environments such as elderhostels or tours sponsored by groups such as museums or an association that a travel agent might not know about?

❑ Are all costs included in the price?

❑ Is a package the best deal for me or would it be less expensive to buy the hotel and fare separately?

❑ What is the composition of the tour?

❑ How much of the tour is structured and how much is free time?

❑ Does the tour require much physical exertion?

❑ Is there any reimbursement if I don't go on all the planned events?

❑ How many meals are included in the tour? If I have special dietary concerns can they be met?

❑ What types of accommodations are provided?

❑ Does the tour need a certain number of people to be viable?

❑ If the tour is canceled, is all my money reimbursed or it the tour rescheduled? What if I can't go when it is rescheduled?

❑ What costs are incurred if I need to cancel?

❑ Should I purchase travel insurance?

Volunteer Vacations

❑ Might I like to help out in another city or country?

❑ What would I like to do—work in the outdoors, do research, build houses, help out in a clinic, go on an archaeological dig?

❑ What countries might benefit most from my skills? Are there organizations that match people with my skills to a country?

❑ What are the costs? Do I get room and board or do I need to pay additional fees? Can I earn college credit for this program?

Courier Travel

❑ Do I want to consider courier travel, where I accompany a package, if I can get a reduced airfare?

❑ Am I free to travel at the last minute?

❑ Are there specific countries where I would prefer to go?

❑ Do they guarantee that what I am carrying is legal in the country that I am traveling to?

❑ How are problems handled?

❑ Will someone meet me when I get to the destination or will I need to deliver the package?

Trip Specifics

Planning the Details of the Trip

❑ Do I have enough identification with me? Is it certified? Do I have a photo ID? Do I have all my reservation confirmation numbers?

❑ Do I have the health and other insurance documents I need?

❑ Do I need additional insurance such as health, travel, trip cancellation, car? Will a health policy cover preexisting conditions? Does my existing car and health insurance cover me where I will be traveling? Will I be able to use my credit card if I am in a car accident or need medical care?

❏ If I am meeting people, do we have a back-up plan in case something happens?

❏ How soon should I get to the airport before departure?

❏ Is it easy to park at the airport? How much extra time do I need to allow if I am parking a car?

❏ How many pieces of luggage may I bring? What are the size requirements or limitations?

❏ Can I check my luggage at the curb or must I check them at the counter?

❏ Do I have a checklist of everything I need to bring?

❏ Have I made all the necessary arrangements at home such as informing neighbors I'll be gone; stopping or arranging for pick up of mail, circulars, and all newspapers including local papers; having plants watered; leaving or having lights turned on?

❏ Is the mass transit system accessible for me if I am disabled?

❏ Will I need additional transportation when I arrive?

❏ Will I need extra money for tolls, tips, departure tax, any other hidden costs?

Renting a Car

❏ What is the confirmation number for this reservation? What name is the reservation under? What is the cancellation policy?

❏ If I decide I want to upgrade, how much more expensive will it be if I upgrade at my destination?

❏ Who can drive the car besides me? What is the minimum age for drivers? Is there an extra fee for additional drivers? Do they have to sign any forms?

❏ Where do I call if my rental car breaks down? How quickly will they respond? If a car breaks down will you provide me with another one?

Going to Another Country

❑ Do I need a visa?

❑ Have I allowed enough time to get a passport or visa? What are the requirements to obtain them?

❑ Do any of the countries I am traveling to require a minimum amount of time be remaining on my passport regardless of how long I plan on staying? [For example, Bali requires that more than six months be remaining on your passport to enter the country.]

❑ Does my health insurance cover me in other countries?

❑ Should I take any special health precautions to visit this destination? Are there any epidemics? Do I need any preventive shots for cholera or malaria or some other contagious disease? Do I have to be careful with any types of food or water?

❑ Is there anything else I should know about potential hazards in this location?

❑ Is there a high rate of crime against tourists?

❑ If I am taking a minor to another country, have I obtained written permission from both parents? If I am divorced and taking my own child, do I have written permission from the child's other parent?

❑ Do I need to reconfirm my travel reservations in the countries I will be visiting? How many days before my departure?

❑ Where do I go and who do I call if I have a problem in another country?

❑ Is there a U.S. embassy in the country that will provide assistance if I have a problem such as losing a passport or if there is political unrest?

❑ Will there be problems making or receiving calls from this country? What is the best way to make phone calls back home? Will it be easy to get a long distance operator from my own carrier? Is there a cheaper way for me to make calls? What can I do if I have problems making or receiving calls? (Your long distance carrier can help with these questions.)

❏ If I am going to be traveling from country to country, do the number and size of my baggage meet the criteria of the different airlines and transportation that I will be using?

❏ Do I need a converter or adapter plugs? What about other necessities such as toilet paper?

❏ What cultural or geographical differences do I need to know about? How formal is the culture? Do I need to dress formally or is casual dress okay? What laws or rules should I be aware of? What are the local customs about tipping?

❏ Am I planning on shopping in other countries? Do I know the prices of what I want to buy? Are there other stores besides airport duty-free shops? Do clothing sizes mean the same there as in my country?

❏ Can I take my computer or other technology with me to this country? Do I need to register what I want to take at the U.S. Customs office to ensure I can bring it back with me?

❏ If I am renting a car in another country, does it have an automatic or manual transmission? What is the price for each? What are the driving rules in the country? What side of the road do they drive on? May I turn right on red lights? Where are the turn signals, lights, and other equipment located in this car? Do I need to keep my headlights on? What type of roads might I encounter in my travels?

Money

❏ Can I count on getting local currency immediately upon arrival or should I bring some with me?

❏ Should I take cash or traveler's checks with me? How easy will it be to use traveler's checks where I go? Will they accept traveler's checks in the shops and outdoor markets? Will I need to pay a fee to cash traveler's checks?

❏ What is the economic situation in the country I am going to?

❏ What is the rate of exchange?

❏ Do I get a better rate of exchange locally or in the country where I am going?

❑ Might I get a better exchange for cash or using a credit card?

❑ What are the rates and commissions charged at banks? Currency exchanges? Hotels?

❑ What hours can I exchange money or traveler's checks?

❑ Should I take a pocket calculator or some type of money converter system with me to determine the rate of exchange?

❑ Do I need an international card, or is my automated teller card sufficient to obtain cash in the countries I'm visiting? Does my bank have a list of the countries that have machines compatible with my card?

❑ Is it better to change my currency back overseas or locally?

❑ Can I get my taxes (on shopping, services, food, and hotel) back when I leave the country I am visiting?

During Travel

❑ If I arrive at the airport early, is there an earlier flight or better connection I can take?

❑ Am I willing to be bumped from my flight? Is the airline asking for volunteers? If I am bumped what will I receive? When is the next flight I can take? Am I guaranteed a place on that plane?

DON'T FORGET

❑ Don't give up doing what is really important to you; you will be angry at yourself and others.

❑ Stay objective about change and possible turmoil.

❑ Don't let another person wreck your day or plans. Enjoy yourself!

❑ When you buy clothing in a foreign country, make sure it fits.

❑ Remove old travel tags so your baggage has only your immediate destination on it.

❑ Look carefully all ways when crossing the street in other countries.

❑ When renting a car determine the size first; upgrading when you get there can be more expensive than initially ordering a larger car. Fill the gas yourself; do not buy the gas option.

❑ Keep credit card receipts for potential tax rebates and to ensure you are properly charged.

❑ Write or call the various tourism organizations for information in the areas that interest you.

❑ Check travel guides such as AAA books, Michelin, Fodor, or others.

❑ Use on-line systems like CompuServe to get travel information and useful tips.

❑ Look for specific books to meet your needs, such as: *Wheelchair Through Europe* by Annie Mackin, available from Graphic Language Press, P.O. Box 270, Cardiff by the Sea, CA 92007.

❑ Investigate current magazines such as *Cruise Travel* for bargains.

❑ Research volunteer opportunities. Some resources are: *Volunteer Vacations* (Chicago Review Press, 1-800-888-4741), *Helping Out in the Outdoors* (American Hiking Society, 703–255–9304), *Environmental Vacations* (John Muir Publications), and *Volunteers for Israel* (330 W. 42nd Street, Suite 1818, New York, NY 10036–6902, 212–643–4848).

❑ To learn about air courier opportunities, contact the International Association of Air Travel Couriers, 8 S. J Street, P.O. Box 1349, Lake Worth, FL 33460, 407-586-0978.

❑ For any questions about what you can take out of or bring back to the country, contact a U.S. customs office near you or the Office of Export Enforcement, U.S. Department of Commerce, P.O. Box 273, Washington, DC 20044, 202–377–4811.

❑ If you have complaints about your mode of travel contact:

Planes:

❑ Federal Aviation Administration, 1-800-322-7873.

❏ U.S. Department of Transportation, C-75, Washington, DC 20590, 202-366-2220.

Ships:

❏ Federal Maritime Commission, Office of Informal Inquiries and Complaints, 1100 L Street, N.W., Washington, DC 20573, 202-523-5807.

Trains:

❏ Amtrak Customer Relations, Washington Union Station, 60 Massachusetts Avenue, N.E., Washington, DC 20002, 202-906-2121.

❏ Federal Railroad Administration, Passenger Programs Division, 400 Seventh Street, S.W., Room 5411, Washington, DC 20590.

Buses:

❏ Regional Compliance Officer, Interstate Commerce Commission, Xerox Center, 55 W. Monroe Street, Suite 550, Chicago, IL 60603–5003, 312-353-6204.

Selecting Lodging

I was planning an out-of-town business trip. Since I would have some free hours, I decided to choose a hotel with a swimming pool. I thought I asked all the right questions, but when I went to swim I discovered the pool was open only early morning and early evening. Even if it were open I wouldn't have been able to swim because the pool was much too small. *Lessons learned:* Probe deeper to make sure that what you need is what they have. Ask about specifics that are important to you: hours the facilities are open, size of the pool, or type of exercise equipment.

There are several options for lodging, including hostels, bed and breakfasts, dormitories, inns, time-shares, motels, hotels, and more. In addition to cost, the location, ambiance, friendliness of staff, your needs, and the reason for your trip may determine the best option for you.

Ask Yourself and Your Traveling Companion

❑ Have we thought about all our alternatives: hotels, time-shares, inns, bed and breakfasts, house swapping, hostels, and campgrounds?

❑ What are we willing to spend on lodging?

❑ What kinds of facilities and services are important to us? Do we want a pool, athletic facilities, massage, hair salon, fax, copy machines, cable, pay TV with movies, VCRs and video rental, restaurants, meals, banquet facilities, meeting rooms, equipment such as overhead projector, flip charts, no-smoking rooms and areas, cooking facilities, playground, children's activities, cribs, high chairs, children's menus, child-care services, facilities to accommodate people with special needs, facilities for a pet? If there are extra charges for these facilities or services, are we willing to pay them?

❑ What kind of location do we want to be in? Do we want easy access to public transportation?

When Making the Reservation

❑ What are the lowest rates I can get? Do you give discounts to members of AAA, CompuServe or other computer networks, AARP, corporations, any other groups? Do you honor coupons? Do you have rates based on the reason for my travel (funeral, wedding, or conference)?

❑ Is this the cheapest rate I can get (after you have been quoted a price)? Are these rates guaranteed?

❑ Do you accept credit cards? Which ones?

❑ What are your room cancellation policies?

❑ What is my reservation number? What is your name?

❑ What are taxes and surcharges in addition to the quoted rates?

❑ Do you have the facilities and services I want?

❑ What are the specifics about the facilities that interest me, such as size of pool?

❑ What hours are these facilities open and available?

❑ Are there no-smoking and smoking rooms?

❑ What kind of environment is the lodging set in? Is it convenient to what I care about?

❑ Will I need a car to get around or is what I want in walking distance? Does the lodging provide transportation?

❑ What will a cab from the airport or point of arrival cost? Do you offer complimentary transportation from my point of arrival to your establishment?

❑ Are there any special events during the time that I will be there that would limit my use of the facilities or take longer to check in? If I want to participate in these events, may I? Do I need reservations?

❑ Do meals come with the accommodations? Are there restaurants in the facility or nearby? Is there easy access to the restaurants?

❑ Are the rooms heated and air conditioned? Can the temperature be controlled in the room?

❑ Are there bathtubs and showers in my room?

❑ Is it a fairly safe area? Should I have any specific concerns?

Ask When Checking In

❑ Is the room located in a quiet area (if quiet is important to you)? Are there any large groups within hearing distance that may cause extra noise?

❑ Are there any rooms with a view?

❑ How far is this room from the elevator? Will I have a long walk? Will I hear the elevator every time it opens?

❑ Who has access to my room? Do you have electronic keys to protect against entry into my room?

❑ What are the fees for using the phones? Are local calls free?

❑ Do you have safety deposit boxes?

❑ What time is checkout? Can I get a later time?

Selecting a Hostel

❑ Do I need a membership? How much does it cost? What is the length of the membership? How will it benefit me? If I am a member, can I reserve a space? Will I receive a room discount?

❏ What is provided and what do I need to bring?

❏ Are there room options? How many people to a room? What is the cost of each option?

❏ How do you assign rooms? Are they segregated by gender?

❏ Is there a limit to how long I can stay?

❏ Might it be hard to get a room? Can I make reservations?

❏ What are the bathroom arrangements and how many people share the facilities?

Selecting a Bed and Breakfast

❏ What sleeping arrangements are offered?

❏ Is there a private bath?

❏ Are showers available?

❏ Do you accept credit cards? What form of payment do you prefer?

❏ How many meals are included? What time are they served? Is there an option to eat in my room?

❏ Are there choices at mealtime? Can special dietary needs be accommodated?

❏ Is there privacy?

❏ Are the mattresses firm (or whatever you prefer)?

Selecting a Cruise Ship

❏ What type of clientele will be present on the cruise, such as children or seniors? Do you cater to a certain clientele?

❏ What is the weather usually like this time of year?

❏ Are there special activities for different groups such as children of different ages?

❏ What type of lodging and location on the ship are available and which would best meet my needs? What is the cost of each option?

❑ How old is the ship? Is it well kept?

❑ Are there plans to retire this ship soon?

Home Swapping

❑ Might I like to swap homes for a vacation?

❑ What type of environment would I like to be in?

❑ Is my geographic location desirable?

❑ Will I allow children or pets to stay in my home?

❑ Have I allowed myself enough time to check references and communicate with the other party?

❑ If in a different country, have I checked my assumptions? Do they have the same conveniences we have?

❑ Are there problems with rodents or insects?

❑ Have I told the people I'm swapping with everything they need to know about being here? Have I clarified my expectations of them and theirs of me? Who pays if appliances break down?

❑ Have I and they left clear instructions on how to use appliances and what to do in case of emergencies?

❑ Have we exchanged tips on the best places to shop, eat, see good entertainment, special events, special offerings?

❑ Have I provided a place for them to store clothes?

❑ Have we made foolproof plans for getting the keys?

Time-Share

❑ Should I invest in a time-share unit?

❑ Would I like to take vacations traveling at the same time and to the same place each year?

❑ Does the complex have flexible use plans?

❑ Do I get the same unit each time?

❑ How easy is it to obtain financing for these units?

❑ Are there any tax advantages?

❑ Will it save me money over time? Are there closing costs? Broker's fees?

❑ What are the annual maintenance fees? How much have fees changed over the years? Do the owners foresee any major expenses that will change the fees?

❑ What types of exchanges are available if I buy a unit and want to go elsewhere? How easy is it to trade a unit where I might like to go? How much in advance will I need to book it? What limitations are there?

❑ Can I rent the unit out myself?

❑ How long have the owners been in business? Are they reputable? Have they been involved in lawsuits? How have they resolved disputes? Will they provide me with references?

❑ What are the chances of reselling the unit? Who handles re-sales?

❑ Is the company willing to put all agreements in the contract?

❑ If the complex is now being built, what guarantee is there that it will be completed on time? Are the builders willing to put my money in escrow until the property is finished?

❑ Does the contract contain provisions in case the builder or management company has financial problems? Am I guaranteed the right of use while any disagreements are resolved?

❑ Do I get to keep ownership rights if the property is bought out?

❑ Can I rent a unit to see if I like the facility?

DON'T FORGET

❑ Get referrals from friends, CompuServe, or other informational networks.

❑ Check lodging ratings in the AAA book or other travel guides.

❑ Read about the type of lodging you are considering.

❑ Check the room before you sign for it.

❑ To get a youth hostel membership call your nearest council travel office (they specialize in student, youth, and budget travelers) or call 1-800-226-8624.

❑ For programs for full-time students, call the Council on International Education Exchange, 1-800-641-2433.

❑ For international volunteer programs open to everyone, write or call the Council on International Educational Exchange, 205 E. 42nd Street, New York, NY 10017, 1-800-468-5562.

❑ A home-swapping service is Intervack International U.S. Home Exchange Service, P.O. Box 590504, San Francisco, CA 94159, 1-800-756-HOME or 1-414-435-3497.

❑ To research time-shares, check with your local real estate commission or attorney general's office.

PART TWO

Settling In

Selecting a
Community

We bought our first home when we got married, in a neighborhood with older children. When our children were born we wanted them to have neighborhood playmates and a more progressive school district, so we began looking into other communities. We found a new home development where young families were building. It was an ideal location, across from a park, in a small school district.

Playmates for our children and the school were top priorities. I hadn't thought much about my likes and dislikes. Within a very short time I learned too many kids can be as unappealing as too few kids. Soon, our school district merged with a larger district and lost some of its benefits. I also discovered that I was a city person who liked sidewalks, big old trees, proximity to the several Minneapolis lakes, and more diverse neighbors. *Lessons learned:* Be clear about what you like and what your family will need for the short and the long term. Know what is really important to you; set your priorities and realistically assess how long they will be important. Investigate community plans to make sure that the benefits that attracted you aren't going to be changed soon.

Ask Yourself and Any People Who Will Be Living with You

❏ What are our first considerations and priorities in selecting a community?

❏ If geographic choices are to be made, what type of climate do we prefer?

❏ Do we want an urban, suburban, or rural community? What type of culture and values do we want in a community?

❏ How important are friendliness, privacy, sense of community, and the celebration of diversity to us?

❏ How close do we want to be, in miles and time, to our workplace, recreation, religious institutions, shopping, activities, health clubs, entertainment, and schools?

❏ How close do we want to be to public transportation?

❏ Do we want to be able to connect to carpools?

❏ Are we concerned about children's needs? Senior citizen needs? Any other type of needs?

❏ Do we want to have more diversity in our neighborhood?

❏ Do we want to be active in a community?

❏ Do we want a neighborhood where people count their neighbors as friends, are relatively friendly, or keep to themselves?

About Children's Needs

❏ Are there many children our children's ages in the community?

❏ What types of schools are available?

❏ If there are options, how difficult is it to get into the school of our choice? What type of waiting list exists? What percentage of the applicants get accepted? What qualifications and criteria is it looking for? Do children from specific neighborhoods get in first?

❑ Has the school our child seeks to attend won any awards?

❑ Have there been problems at this school? If so, what type?

❑ What is the average class size and the teacher-to-student ratio?

❑ What are the school's teaching and learning philosophies?

❑ Is there bus service to the school? How long is the bus ride? Are there late-activity buses?

❑ What types of extracurricular programs exist? Is there a fee for programs?

❑ If needed, does the school have extended-day programming? Does it serve breakfast, snacks, and other meals? What activities are offered in extended day? Are there summer programs?

❑ What community activities exist for children? Are there sport teams for both boys and girls? Are classes offered such as drama, arts and crafts, computer, or other desired activities?

❑ Are there parks and park programs in the community? What are the park facilities? Are there classes or organized activities in the park? Who is in charge of the programs? Who is in charge of the children?

❑ What are curfews for youth?

❑ Do safe homes exist where children can go in emergencies? Do homes have signs that show they are safe homes? How well screened are the safe homes?

About the City or Community

❑ What public transportation exists in this community?

❑ Is it easy to use?

❑ How often does it run during the week and on the weekend?

❑ How much does it cost?

❑ What opportunities are there for community involvement? How do I get involved?

❑ What types of task forces or commissions exist? How are members selected?

❑ What are the procedures to follow if I have a concern I want addressed?

❑ Does the community have truth-in-housing laws that require a building inspection for any house being sold? Can I, as a buyer, see the report? Is there a code of compliance that requires the seller to fix any problems before the house is sold?

❑ Are there community offerings such as senior programs or adult education?

❑ What are long-term plans for this community regarding schools, parks, assessments, the elderly?

❑ Is there a demographic report that talks about the present community and predicts future trends?

❑ Are there anticipated new costs or charges that I should know about?

❑ What kind of garbage collection is provided? What does it cost? How often is it collected?

❑ What types of recycling programs exist? Are there cost benefits for me?

❑ Do some areas have neighborhood involvement groups? Which ones? What do they do?

❑ Do some areas have crime watch programs? Which ones?

❑ Does the community have an Operation I.D. program?

❑ What are the crime statistics in this community? In specific neighborhoods? Do the police have crime prevention programs in the community?

❑ Will insurance (car, homeowner) cost more in this community?

❑ Where and when do I register to vote? Where do I vote?

❑ What licenses or permits do I need—dog, bicycle, fishing and hunting, building? Can I get them at city hall? Where do I go for licenses not provided at city hall?

❑ Have there been any problems with drinking water in this community?

❑ When does the community test sirens?

❑ Is there a limit on how often I can have a garage sale?

❑ Are there any animal problems such as raccoons?

❑ What kinds of social services are provided in this community?

❑ Are there specific areas in the community where there is heavy traffic? Heavy air traffic noise? Railroad tracks?

DON'T FORGET

❑ Call local organizations such as the League of Women Voters to see if they have or know of any reports discussing issues faced by this specific community.

❑ Call the local community paper and ask any questions you may have.

❑ Drive through the neighborhoods and notice how neat and well groomed the areas are, whether the streets and curb areas are clean, whether there are any open drainage ditches, and other community-upkeep concerns.

❑ Attend a city council or special-interest task force meeting.

❑ Visit a religious institution that may interest you to ask questions and meet the congregation.

❑ Ask to see a police report.

❑ Talk to realtors about the community.

Renting a Residence

Susan and John recently rented their first apartment in their ideal neighborhood. Soon after they settled in, a restaurant opened across the street. It had outdoor seating and drew many people to the neighborhood. Susan needed to rise early for her job and the noise disturbed her into the night. In addition, garbage pickup was early in the morning on her only morning off. They thought they were moving into a quiet neighborhood and instead found excessive noise. *Lessons learned:* Ask the city planning department about plans for businesses or new developments in the neighborhood and how you might be affected. Ask about early-morning or late-night noises and garbage pickup. Ask about and experience the noise level in the unit you want.

People choose to rent for various reasons: low maintenance, flexibility, can't afford to or don't want to own. If you would rather buy than rent, check out all your options. Some financing requires just a minimal down payment. If you can afford to buy but don't want to own, make sure you understand the financial ramifications of your decision.

There are times when renters can call the shots and times when it is hard to find an apartment. If it is a renter's market, try to get the best deal you can. Sometimes you can get an extra month or two free, free parking, or other benefits.

Ask Yourself and Your Housemate

❑ Would we prefer to be near or in an urban, suburban, or rural area?

❑ Do we want to take care of property or have no responsibilities for the upkeep?

❑ Do we want to rent a house, apartment, or condominium?

❑ How much space do we want? What is the minimum acceptable?

❑ Do we want it furnished?

❑ Do we want land or extra space for gardening, hobbies, or any other activities?

❑ Do we want room for entertaining?

❑ Do we want amenities such as an exercise facility, pool, party room, washer and dryer?

❑ What kind of parking arrangements do we want?

❑ Do we want to have a pet?

❑ How much are we willing to pay?

❑ How much up-front money can we afford?

❑ Do we want to sign a one-year lease, a six-month lease, or rent month to month?

❑ Have we asked each other all the questions we need to in order to live together?

❑ Have we been honest with each other about our needs and idiosyncrasies?

❑ Have we worked through potential problem areas?

Ask Landlords

❑ How much money do we need to put down?

❑ If there is a security deposit, what are the requirements to get the deposit back? After vacating the premises, how quickly is the deposit returned?

❑ Will you be shampooing the carpet, repainting, and finishing other maintenance work before we move in?

❑ Is parking available? Is it covered? Underground? Is parking assigned or open? How much extra? Is there a waiting list? How long a wait?

❑ Is there easy access to off-street parking? Are there alternate days for parking or other rules I should know about?

❑ Is there ample guest parking?

❑ Have there been crimes committed in this neighborhood? In this building?

❑ How secure is the building? Do you change keys and locks when tenants move out? Do you require a criminal background check on any building staff who may have access to the apartment?

❑ What is the shortest or longest lease we can sign? Are there clauses for subletting? Under what circumstance can you or I terminate the lease?

❑ What is the noise level in this unit? Is it possible to hear outside noises and other tenants?

❑ What type of rules exist in this building? How many people are allowed to live in one unit? Are late-night parties allowed?

❑ What is the profile of the other tenants?

❑ Is there an on-site caretaker? How quickly does the caretaker tend to problems in the apartment? Will we have to pay to fix anything or are all repairs included?

❑ How often are the common areas cleaned?

❑ How often are the units painted, carpets cleaned, appliances replaced?

❑ Are there extra costs for the amenities? How easily can the amenities be accessed and used? What are the busy hours?

❑ How do you dispose of garbage and trash?

❑ What monthly and upkeep costs are the tenants expected to pay?

❑ What are the average utility costs for this unit?

❑ Do you allow pets? What kind? Is there a size limit?

❑ Is barbecuing allowed on the balcony?

❑ Do you have a rodent or bug problem? Do you exterminate? How often? Do you pay for all the costs?

❑ Has there been a history of maintenance or structural problems in this building? If so, what were they and how were they repaired?

❑ Is there an option for terminating the lease early?

❑ Do you anticipate selling this property soon?

❑ Are you willing to sign a contract that includes all the details you told me?

About Insurance

❑ What does the landlord's property insurance cover?

❑ If someone falls in my apartment, is my guest covered by the landlord's insurance?

❑ In case of a fire, tornado, or other disaster, is my property covered by the landlord's insurance?

❑ Do I need renters' insurance?

❑ What will it cover?

❑ What kind of deductibles are there?

❑ Is there limited coverage on specific items such as computers, musical instruments, or bikes?

❑ If something is stolen or damaged do I get its replacement value or the amount I originally paid back?

❑ Can I apply for insurance with my roommates?

❑ Is my property covered if I am away from home?

❑ Can I get a lower insurance rate if I am a nonsmoker? Own a fire extinguisher? If I take specific security measures?

DON'T FORGET

❑ Note how easy it is to contact the rental agent or caretaker to view the apartment. If you have a difficult time reaching the person, it may not be easy to get repairs tended to quickly.

❑ Watch the disposition of the person that shows the apartment. Is she friendly and cordial? If it's the same person who will be tending to problems, you want to make sure that she seems helpful.

❑ Take a good look at the cleanliness of the common areas, including the laundry room.

❑ Pay attention to the noise level in the area when you are viewing the unit.

❑ Observe other tenants when you are visiting the unit.

❑ Talk to present tenants about the unit. Get their impressions about living in the building.

❑ Read the contract carefully. Make sure it clarifies all the points you asked about and specifies all the details you were told and any other stipulations you may want in the contract.

❑ Make sure the details you agree upon, even appliance replacement and maintenance, are in writing.

❑ Make sure you see the exact unit you will be renting.

❑ Check with the police to see how many noise complaints have been reported from this residence. Ask them about crime incidents reported from tenants in the building.

❑ Check with a rental service about the history and reputation of the apartment building.

❑ Look into renting a condominium. They may be more appealing because the tenants are long term. Check with rental services and newspaper ads. Ask what percentage of the building may be rented out.

❑ If you want quiet try to find corner units, a unit on the top floor, or a townhouse.

❑ Check the lighting in and outside the building at night.

❑ Visit the apartment at a time when most people are home to check the noise level, parking availability, and more.

❑ Note the condition of the apartment. Write down with the owner any preconditions to ensure you are not held responsible for someone else's damage.

❑ If you have questions or concerns regarding tenants' rights, find out if your state has a tenants union or call your city hall for help.

❑ If you feel you have been denied housing, contact the Office of Fair Housing and Equal Opportunity, U.S. Department of Housing and Urban Development, Room 5204, Washington, DC 20410–2000; your state human rights department; your city's housing department; and the local human rights commission. Your community may have an agency that deals with unfair housing practices.

Selecting a Real Estate Agent

When I bought my present home, I was overwhelmed by problems. I understood that an agent can't know all there is to know about a home, yet I didn't expect to be left alone to handle the problems. I warned my agent that I did not trust the selling agent, who had a bad reputation. My agent said she could handle her. To make matters worse, the sellers had moved out of state and their selling agent was taking care of any requirements necessary to sell the house.

One thing that needed to be fixed prior to closing was the roof flashing (the waterproofing sheet metal). The selling agent reported that the flashing had been repaired. Soon after I acquired the house, a roof leak made it clear the problem hadn't been solved. I discovered that a handyman who had never repaired a flat roof had done the work. I believe a good agent should protect interests, know the key questions to ask, and help if you do get stuck.

Lessons learned: If you buy from out-of-state sellers you can't take them to small claims court, so it is harder and more costly to get disputes resolved. Learn if the agent you are selecting helps resolve problems after the closing and will share costs. Ask about the qualifications of people who work on your house. Trust your gut. If you know an agent that represents the other party has a bad reputation, go over everything with a fine-tooth comb.

There are various work arrangements for real estate agents. They may be affiliated with a national company, a local company, a franchise, or be independent. There are benefits to working with each type of agent. National affiliations may expand the exposure of your house if you are the seller, larger offices may have more support, and independents may be freer to negotiate fees. Different types of agencies attract realtors with varying degrees of experience. An agent who has sold many homes may be attractive to you; newer agents who are trying to prove themselves may give you more attention. Explore your options, interview people, and ask candid questions before you make a decision.

Ask Yourself

❑ What is most important to me as I select an agent?

❑ Am I willing to pay full commission, or do I want an agent who will discount fees?

❑ Is it important to me whether an agent is part of a national network?

❑ Do I want an agent who has sold a lot of homes in my area?

❑ What are my expectations of an agent?

Ask Potential Agents

❑ What are your qualifications, education, and training? How long have you been selling real estate? What is your expertise? Why should I choose to work with you?

❑ Have there been circumstances when you made a mistake or misinformed clients? What were the circumstances and how did you resolve them?

❑ What services does your firm provide? Will your firm buy my home if I can't sell it? Do you have some type of warranty program?

❑ Do you qualify buyers before you show them the property?

❑ How well do you know the community I want to live in or sell in?

❑ What do you see as the benefits to owning a home in this community?

❑ How many homes have you listed and sold in my community? In the community I am interested in living in?

❑ How well do you understand structural issues? Can you spot potential problems?

❑ If you find a buyer, will you represent my interests, the buyer's interests, or your own best interest?

❑ Have you had complaints filed against you? How were they handled and who handled them?

❑ What professional associations do you belong to?

❑ How reachable are you? What is your policy on returning phone calls?

❑ Do you have an assistant that I will be working with?

When You're the Seller

❑ How do I know that you will obtain the best deal for me?

❑ If the home I want to buy is also listed by your agency, is there a conflict of interest for your agency? What happens in that case?

❑ How will you determine the price of my home? Do you check similar houses that sell in my area? Will you show me the data that influenced your pricing decisions?

❑ What is your commission? Are you free to negotiate it?

❑ Will you sign a nonexclusive agreement so I can sell my house by myself if the opportunity presents itself?

❑ What is the minimum time I can contract with you?

❑ Are you willing to assist with any costs or demands that may arise in the selling of my home in order to make a sale?

❑ How will you market my home? Do you contact or hold open houses for other realtors? Will you advertise my home in the newspaper? Are you part of a national network? Do you use direct mail? Do you take pictures or prepare a visual presentation of my home for prospective buyers? Who pays for this advertising?

❑ Will you assist in getting my home ready for sale? How will you help?

❑ What kind of signage do you use? Is it eye catching?

❑ Will you leave information describing my home outside for pedestrians and people who are driving by? How often do you check to ensure handouts are available?

❑ Do you display detailed information in my home for prospective buyers?

❑ Do you have a twenty-four-hour number if people want information about the home?

When You're the Buyer

❑ For each home you recommend, may I see a visual presentation of it first to determine if I want to tour the house?

❑ What happens if I buy a home and have unexpected problems? Do you help me? How often does this happen? How have you helped other clients?

❑ May I call clients you have sold to?

❑ Do you know many agents who sell homes in this area?

❑ Are there special programs that may grant me a mortgage?

❑ Do you participate in HUD sales programs?

❑ Do you have relationships with mortgage brokers?

DON'T FORGET

❑ Ask friends, co-workers, and neighbors to recommend a good agent.

❑ When selling your home, ask a few agents to do a market evaluation of your property. This process will help you assess them.

❑ Drive through your area and see if one company or agent is getting more listings than others.

❑ Attend open houses and visit with realtors.

❑ Make sure you feel comfortable with the realtor you hire.

❑ Make sure the realtor asks about your needs, listens to you, and shows you homes that fit your needs.

❑ Be wary if your agent says he has never made a mistake.

❑ If you are moving out of town you might want to use a referral service. If you know reputable agents in your old community, ask them for help.

❑ Check with your state's realty association to learn about local professional organizations. Does your realtor belong? Has he had cases arbitrated? Was he cooperative in past arbitration?

Buying a Home

I hesitated about buying my present home because it had a detached garage; I really wanted an attached two-car garage. My realtor said, "You can just add one." I discovered after I bought the house that adding on was no easy task. First of all, the house had a strange roof line; contractors emphasized it would be a complicated and expensive job. Second, a double-car garage wouldn't conform to codes. I would have to ask for a city variance, and there was no guarantee it would be approved. *Lessons learned:* Don't believe everything you are told. Check potential changes first to see if they meet codes. If a variance is needed, ask city officials about the likelihood of it being approved and whether a variance has ever been denied. Ask a contractor if what you want is possible, at what cost, and about any potential problems.

Often when we purchase a home we think primarily of our present needs and situation. But needs change, and so do financial circumstances. Consider whether a property you are interested in will meet your changing needs.

You might think you would be willing to give something up to get the best deal, yet the something may be very important to you and will keep you from really enjoying your home. Buying a home is a big decision and should be weighed very carefully.

Ask Yourself

❑ How much money am I willing to spend monthly?

❑ How much of a down payment can I afford?

❑ Will I qualify for a mortgage? How much of a mortgage can I get? Are there any special mortgage programs (such as Fannie Mae, the federal home mortgage agency) I may qualify for?

❑ Will my credit history be acceptable?

❑ Would I prefer a home where I do the maintenance or a home, condominium, or townhouse where the maintenance is provided?

❑ How important is size? Might I prefer an older or smaller home in a certain neighborhood? Am I willing to move to a different neighborhood to get a bigger home?

❑ What type of living space do I want—one floor, two story, split entry, or other floor plan?

❑ What am I willing to give up and what is an absolute necessity? Fireplace? Air conditioning? Finished basement? Adequate storage? Garbage disposal? Dishwasher? Separate dining area? Storage space?

❑ Would I like a new home? Do I want to build a home? Do I want to hire a general contractor or serve as my own contractor and hire subcontractors?

Ask When Purchasing Any Type of Property

❑ How much are the closing costs? Additional costs?

❑ How strict or lax were the building codes when this property was built?

❑ How have the building codes changed since this property was built?

❑ Are there any encumbrances against this property?

❑ Are there any assessments, either present or anticipated, on this property?

❑ What stays with the home? Appliances? Window treatments? Special fixtures?

❑ Have there been any water problems? If yes, how have they been fixed?

❑ Does the residence have safety features? Is there a security system? If so, is it monitored? Is there a fire alarm in working condition? Are the doors strong? How are the windows? Are they easy to access? Is there a way of seeing who is at the door without opening the door? Are there deadbolt locks on the doors and good locks on any sliding glass doors?

❑ If there is undeveloped land nearby, how will it be developed? Might it be zoned commercial?

❑ Does the undeveloped land serve a purpose such as water drainage that might change and affect my property in any way?

❑ How easy will it be to resell this property?

Ask When Selecting a Condominium or Planned Community

❑ What is the noise level in this unit?

❑ What codes and rules do I have to follow?

❑ Can I rent my unit out? Is there a limited percentage of the units that can be rented? How many are rented now? Might the percentage of rentals affect my ability to get a mortgage?

❑ Are there association fees? What is the monthly fee? What is included in this fee? How much have they increased over the years? How often have they been increased? What influences this fee? Are changes in the fee structure anticipated soon?

❑ Are pets allowed? What kind? Is there a size limitation?

❑ How does one become involved in the homeowner's association?

❑ Is barbecuing allowed on the balcony?

❑ If a planned community, are there any restrictive covenants? Do I have freedom or limitations regarding house colors, shrubs, mailboxes, swimming pool, porches, fences, cars or boats parked in the driveway, free-standing sheds?

Ask When Purchasing an Existing Home

❑ Are there existing city codes that limit changes that can be made to the house?

❑ What is the process to apply for a city variance if my change doesn't meet existing codes? How long does it take for a hearing? Have there been previous hearings on this property? If yes, what has been the outcome? What is the likelihood of this variance being approved?

❑ What types of remodeling do I need permits for?

❑ How old is the roof? Furnace? Water softener? Other appliances? Have they been repaired?

❑ When was the house last painted? How often has it needed to be painted?

❑ How much is the average electric bill? Gas bill? Water bill?

❑ How often does the lawn need to be mowed?

❑ Is there a vacuum breaker on all outside faucets and the laundry tub so the drinking water is safe?

❑ How is the drainage around the foundation of the home?

❑ Are there ample electrical outlets to use my appliances and other electrical products?

❑ When can I assume occupancy? If this date needs to be changed, are you willing to cover any costs I may have such as a motel?

DON'T FORGET

❑ Pay an independent home inspector to look over the house. The money that you spend now could save you a lot more in the future.

❑ Look carefully at ceilings, floors, and walls for signs of water damage in any house you are considering.

❑ Get a copy of your credit report to make sure there are no mistakes and that you will qualify for a mortgage.

❑ Shop around for mortgages. Look for lower interest rates and points and the best monthly payment for you.

❑ Ensure the purchase agreement covers small details such as who pays the water, gas, and electric bills up to certain dates. Have this money put in escrow to cover costs.

❑ Make sure that all loose ends are tied up by the closing and that all agreed-upon transactions have occurred.

❑ If the seller has to make repairs before closing, make sure the person hired is well qualified.

❑ Contact the U.S. Department of Housing and Urban Development at 1-800-767-4483 for a free booklet called *Home of Your Own* that explains HUD homes.

❑ For information on developing accessible housing in your area, contact the National Handicapped Housing Institute, 1050 Thorndale Avenue, New Brighton, MN 55112, 612-639-9799.

❑ If you feel you have been denied housing, contact the Office of Fair Housing and Equal Opportunity, U.S. Department of Housing and Urban Development, Room 5204, Washington, DC 20410–2000; your state human rights department; your city's housing department; and the local human rights commission. Your community may have an agency that deals with unfair housing practices.

Ask a Builder or Remodeling Contractor (see also Hiring a Repair Person)

❑ How long have you been in business?

❑ Do you have liability insurance?

❑ Are you willing to make changes in standard plans?

❑ How much do blueprint changes cost?

❑ Do you have an architect to make changes?

❑ Do you do the work yourself or contract out?

❑ What are your qualifications and the qualifications of your subcontractors?

❑ Who will be supervising the project?

❑ If you don't complete the work on schedule and I have to incur costs (such as lodging), are you willing to cover those costs?

❑ Will you provide references I may contact? May I go into some of your completed homes?

❑ Are you planning on staying in this community to build other homes?

❑ What if things don't work right such as the fireplace or glass doors? How quickly will you take care of problems? Will you put that in writing?

❑ What are your building allowances? Do most clients stay within those allowances? What is the average amount that clients spend?

❑ If a new development, what is the profile of other people who are building here?

❑ Why is your bid different from my other bids? Are the materials different? What are the pros and cons of this material?

❑ Do you acquire the proper building permits? Do I have to pay extra for them? What do they cost?

❑ Do you remove all debris from the area?

DON'T FORGET

❑ Get referrals for reputable builders and contractors from friends.

❑ If energy conservation is important to you, call the power company for specialists.

❑ Use building supply stores and hardware stores as a resource for names of contractors.

❑ Check whether they belong to a builders' association or other professional organizations.

❑ Call your local Department of Commerce office to see if they are licensed.

❑ Ask for references and call them. Find out if the work was done on time, if there were hidden costs, what they were happy with and what they were unhappy with.

❑ Get everything in writing, including any changes to initial plans.

❑ Put a holdback clause in your contract that allows you to withhold final payments until you have the job inspected.

❑ Put a clause in a contract protecting you if the contractor doesn't pay his subcontractors.

❑ Tell contractors your expectations—cleaning up after themselves, no smoking in the house, or other important restrictions.

Hiring a Moving Company

Joan used a cheap mover recommended by friends. She hired them over the phone without having them look at all she had to move. She assumed they would have boxes and would help her pack if she needed them to. When they arrived she discovered that they did not have any boxes and they didn't help people pack. Their truck was fairly small and they had to make many trips from the old neighborhood to the new neighborhood. Joan went to the new house and the movers ended up locking themselves out of the old house. Instead of coming back for the key they tried to break into the house. A neighbor reported them to the police and they were detained for questioning. Because they charged by the hour, the cost of the move was much greater than Joan expected. *Lessons learned:* Have a mover come to your home and give you a written estimate. Show them everything you will want them to move, including books and other items that will be boxed. Ask how many trips it will take to move from one house to the other. Ideally have someone at each place of residence. Have a back-up plan in case the movers have a problem.

Sharon ordered a trailer to help her son Aaron move to college. When she went to pick it up, she discovered they didn't have one in stock. After many phone calls, she found a distant location where she could be the next one to get a trailer, but she still had to wait until the next day to pick it up. *Lessons learned*: When renting equipment or a vehicle, ask if it's guaranteed for the time and place you ordered it from.

Ask Yourself

❑ Do I want to rent equipment and a vehicle and move myself? Do I want to load and unload my goods myself but have a company drive the truck to my destination? Do I want a mover to do everything—load, unload, and drive the truck? Do I want the mover to help pack any items? Which items?

❑ Do I want to buy good moving boxes or get used boxes from local stores? What other supplies do I need (marking pens, labels, packing tape, cords, dollies, bubble wrap, newspapers)? Is it less expensive to rent equipment and supplies from a moving company or a specialty store?

❑ Am I moving anything I don't really want or need? Will everything I'm taking fit into my new residence?

❑ Have I labeled the boxes so the movers and I can easily identify the contents? Have I indicated fragile items and noted them on the boxes? Do I want to label the boxes according to which rooms they will go to?

❑ Have I made an inventory of what I am moving, including a box count?

❑ If the movers are packing me and I won't be there, have I left clear instructions about what to pack? Can I find a friend or relative to be there with the movers to answer any questions and give directions?

❑ Does my homeowners' insurance cover damages or loss during a move? Is additional insurance necessary and available?

❑ Is the free limited liability insurance I receive (based on the weight of an item) written into the contract with the movers? Do I want to be better protected with added-value coverage or full-value coverage? What is the difference in cost and protection for these different options?

❑ Is there a deductible?

❑ If moving for a job, are my moving expenses deductible?

❑ If the house I am moving into or from will be unoccupied for any length of time, have I notified neighbors or police?

❑ Am I giving enough notice to turn off or on any services (newspaper, phone, utilities)?

❑ Have I sent change of address cards to magazines? Creditors? Friends?

Ask the Moving Company

❑ How is your rate determined—hours spent, weight of the load, space used on the moving van, distance?

❑ How do you keep track of the hours (if an hourly rate)?

❑ Do you have discount options where I can help load and unload the truck?

❑ Are there extra charges for moving appliances? Pianos? Moving up flights of steps or elevators? Traffic time? Extra stops for loading or unloading? If the van doesn't fit in the driveway?

❑ Are there certain times of the year the moving rate is cheaper?

❑ Do you provide storage? What is the fee? For what length of time?

❑ Do I have to pay more if you pick up and deliver on specific dates? Are you willing to put those times and dates in a written contract?

❑ Do you pay for any expenses I have to incur if you are late? Will you put that in a written contract?

❑ Do you pack and unpack?

❑ Do you unplug and install appliances?

❑ What is the total fee?

❏ Can I know the total cost of the move up front? Do you offer a binding estimate that locks you into a maximum moving price? Is the price lowered if I move less?

❏ Are you bonded?

❏ What happens if anything is lost or damaged during the move?

❏ What procedures are used to handle disputes? Is that written in the contract?

❏ Is there a time limit for claims to be filed? How soon do you pay claims?

❏ Do you participate in the American Movers Arbitration Settlement Program?

❏ When do I need to pay you? What methods of payment do you accept?

❏ Is it expected that I tip the drivers? If so, how much?

❏ Can I leave clothing or other items in drawers?

❏ How is it best to pack fragile items?

❏ Do you provide a written inventory of what you are moving? Are previous scratches or flaws noted in that inventory? Do I see and approve the inventory notations before the move? Will the driver point out flaws or any concerns to me before the object is put on the van?

❏ What is a typical complaint by a client? How is that usually handled?

If You're Moving Out Of Town

❏ If I'm being transferred or taking a new job, will the company provide a moving allowance?

❏ Can the mover guarantee the date my shipment will arrive? If not, how am I informed of the arrival date?

❏ If the moving van gets to the destination before I do, do they hold the shipment? Do they leave it in the van or store it? If they move it twice does that increase the chances of damage? What is the fee for holding it in the van or storage?

❑ Might it be cheaper to send some of my things through the mail or any other means?

❑ Are there some items that won't keep well in the van? What are those? How am I going to move plants? Pets?

❑ Have I obtained or sent all the records (school, medical) that I need?

❑ Do I need to reserve lodging during the move?

❑ Will the mover transport my car? Are there additional costs? What is the procedure? Will my car be fully covered by insurance if something happens to it during the move?

Moving from an Apartment

❑ Can the movers easily get in and out of the building?

❑ Does someone need to be there if the movers have to leave the building doors open?

❑ Is there something I need to do if there will be heavy use of the elevator?

Renting Moving Equipment and Vehicles

❑ Do you have various size trailers, vans, and trucks?

❑ Which size would best meet my needs?

❑ Is there a minimum or maximum rental time?

❑ Am I charged a flat rate or by the mile? Am I allowed more mileage than the exact distance? What are the charges if I exceed the mileage?

❑ If I return it early can I get any money back?

❑ Are there times when lower rates are offered?

❑ Do I need to give a deposit? If so, will it be deducted from my bill?

❑ Is there an additional fee if I am taking it one way?

❑ Does my car insurance cover theft or damage? Do I need additional insurance? How much is it?

❑ Do you have dollies, towing equipment, rope, boxes, and blankets? How much are they to rent or buy? Do I take the equipment with me and return it with the vehicle?

❑ How soon before the move do I need to order the truck?

❑ Am I guaranteed to get the truck at the time and date I have asked for it?

❑ Will it be available at the location I ordered it from or might I have to pick it up at another location?

❑ Is there a drop-off location in the city I am going to? If not, where do I need to return it?

❑ Must I fill up the gas tank before returning the truck or to the same level as when rented? How much do you charge per gallon if I don't fill it up on my own?

❑ What happens if something goes wrong with the vehicle when I am on the road? Will you send someone? How quickly?

DON'T FORGET

❑ Ask for references.

❑ Research specific companies by calling the Better Business Bureau and reading consumer magazines.

❑ Make sure the contract is comprehensive and details all agreements and arrangements. Make sure the mover's liability is clearly stated, including information about boxes you have packed yourself.

❑ Determine how claims are handled if a problem arises and write as much into the contract as possible.

❑ Don't sign a release form for the shipment until you have checked to make sure there are no damages. Look carefully at unboxed items and check your fragile boxes.

❑ Mark any concerns you have on the inventory sheet before you pay.

❑ Don't dispose of broken pieces or damaged items until you have shown them to the moving company.

❑ Binding arbitration, where both parties agree to arbitrate, exists for interstate moves through the American Movers Conference. Arbitration through writing has no fee, but a proceeding with an arbitrator has a small fee. Call your local or regional office of the Interstate Commerce Commission to see if your mover participates in the program. To request arbitration write American Movers Conference, Dispute Settlement Program, 2200 Mill Road, Alexandria, VA 22314 within sixty days after the moving company denies your claim or makes a final offer.

❑ Ask the moving company for any consumer information they may have. In particular, ask for the pamphlet *Your Rights and Responsibilities When You Move*.

❑ Contact the Consumer Education Research Center, 350 Scotland Road, Orange, NJ 07050, 1-800-872-0121 or 201-676-6663 to purchase a book titled *How to Save $$$ On Your Moving Bills*.

Selecting a Pet

Cindy recently purchased a Labrador from the Humane Society. Soon after she bought the dog it required hip surgery, at a cost of $2,000. Labradors are prone to hip problems. Cindy knew this but purchased the dog anyway. For many pet lovers, spending that kind of money would not be feasible.

Pets, like humans, have their good and bad qualities. When you choose, you will need to ask yourself if the good qualities of this pet outweigh the negative qualities. Some pets might be more work but also more fun. It is important to understand the full impact of pet ownership (both the amount of care and expense involved) before you embark on this venture. It will save you time, money, and emotions. *Lessons learned:* Understand the predispositions before you buy an animal. Know the implications of these characteristics.

Ask Yourself

❏ How much time am I willing to spend on a daily basis caring for an animal?

❏ Am I willing to spend time training a pet?

❑ How much money do I want to spend initially, monthly, and over the year on a pet?

❑ What are my expectations for a pet? Do I want affection? Obedience? A companion? A protector? A lap dog? A hunting dog?

❑ What kind of temperament do I want a pet to have? Does it need to be good with children?

❑ Is it important for the animal to have a pedigree? Do I want to show or breed the animal?

❑ Do I want a newborn or older pet?

❑ Do I want a pet that is already housebroken or trained?

❑ Do I want an outdoor pet or a house pet? Will I have areas that are off limit to the pet?

❑ Who is going to care for the pet? If my children are, am I willing to take over if they don't, when they go to college, or leave home?

❑ Since some complexes don't allow animals, am I willing to limit my living choices because I have a pet?

Ask When Purchasing a Pet

❑ Does this breed meet my criteria?

❑ What is the average life of this animal?

❑ What are the common predisposed conditions for this breed?

❑ What type of temperament, genetics, and idiosyncrasies does this animal have?

❑ What special features does this animal have? What is the animal known for?

❑ How much care does this pet require? What specifics do I need to know about caring for this animal?

❑ How much grooming does this animal need? Are there seasons when the animal will need different grooming such as shorter hair?

❑ How much does it cost to groom the animal? Neuter? Declaw? What can potential illness cost?

❑ What ongoing grooming will I need to do?

❑ What kind of dental care does this animal need? What are ongoing dental costs?

❑ What is the probability that extra care and costs will be needed such as cleaning ears more often, spending money on surgery, having a blind animal?

❑ How does the animal interact with children? With strangers?

❑ What is known about the parents? How often do they breed the mother?

❑ If I want to breed or show dogs, can I see the parents?

❑ Are there specific hereditary problems such as seizures, immune disorders, or allergies I should know about? Are there any guarantees that this won't be a problem for this particular animal?

❑ Has the animal received a checkup and shots? Were the animal's eyes checked? Was the animal checked for heart murmurs and other types of conditions?

❑ Do you guarantee your animals?

❑ How large will this specific animal get?

❑ Will this pet fit my lifestyle? For example, if I want to take the dog with me on errands, is she a good traveler?

❑ How easy is it to train this pet? Will I need to take this pet to obedience school? Is this breed receptive to training? What behaviors will I need to tolerate in this animal and what will be obedience issues?

❑ What is the activity level of this animal?

❑ How much exercise does this animal need? Is it okay to exercise the pet in very hot weather?

❑ How much food should this animal have during the day? Are there specific brands of food that are better than others? What about table food and treats?

❑ What additional supplies will I need?

❑ What type of shots does the animal require?

❑ Does this animal shed much?

❑ What is the average life span of this animal?

Ask a Veterinarian and Clinic

❑ Are you board certified?

❑ Where were you trained?

❑ Do you take continuing education courses? How do you stay current in the field?

❑ What associations do you belong to?

❑ How long have you practiced?

❑ Do you specialize in certain kinds of animals?

❑ Do you hire certified veterinary technicians or do you train them yourself?

❑ Is the clinic American Animal Hospital Association certified?

❑ Do you board animals?

❑ Do you keep animals overnight if they have a procedure done?

❑ Do you keep cats and dogs separate?

❑ Can you be reached twenty-four hours a day?

❑ What do I do in case of an emergency? Do you have an emergency service you refer people to?

DON'T FORGET

❑ Research the animal carefully. Get a good breed book, talk to veterinarians, talk to pet owners, meet breeders.

❑ Decide the best place to buy for your needs. Check the Humane Society, pet stores, professional breeders, and backyard breeders.

❑ If you want a show-quality dog, buy from a breeder, and make sure the dog fits breed standards.

❑ Ensure proper tests and credentials are given to you.

PART THREE

A Life's Work

Selecting a
Job or Career

Several years ago I accepted a position as marketing director for a small company. Within the first few days, I discovered there was no budget to do the job. It also became clear early on that two of the top people had business values that conflicted with my values. I quit after three days. Time proved that my instincts were right—the company was sued for fraud. *Lessons learned*: Ask about your budget and staff support. Get a sense of the values of the key people. Go with your gut; being a quitter can be better than staying in a bad situation.

As an organization development consultant I have experienced many work environments. The most common complaint I have heard is lack of clear communication. People often don't know what is expected of them, don't have input when they should, don't get important information, get mixed messages, and hear conflicting reports. It is difficult to produce efficiently and effectively without clarity. *Lessons learned*: Determine whether a potential employer has clear processes and procedures. Ask about internal communication vehicles. How will you learn about factors that affect your job? Ask about employee input.

A former vice president of an international corporation told me about trying to convince someone to accept a big promotion.

He stressed the salary, prestige, and power of the job. It turned out the employee didn't want money, prestige, and power. The vice president said it would have been a lot easier if he had asked what the man valued before launching into his pitch.

It is common to assume others want and value what you do. In a workshop I conducted a few years ago, I asked the twenty participants what it would take for them to feel valued in the workplace. To my surprise there were twenty different answers. *Lessons learned*: We should learn what is important to us and try to find it. We also need to recognize that others may have different priorities. Clear, concise communication is extremely important in locating the right job and employer.

Ask Yourself

❑ What are my personal and professional goals?

❑ What do I want and expect from a career? From an employer?

❑ What are my strengths and weaknesses? Do I work well under pressure? Am I well organized? Am I better at creating, assessing, managing, or implementing?

❑ What working environment do I like best? Do I like people contact, or do I need a quiet work space? Are there certain types of people I work best with?

❑ Do I want structure or flexibility?

❑ Am I a self-starter?

❑ What is the minimum salary necessary to maintain my lifestyle? Am I willing to make changes in my life for a lower salary?

❑ Do I want a set salary, commission, or bonus opportunities?

❑ Do I want a career and employment with opportunities for advancement?

Ask People Who Are in Your Field of Interest

❑ What do you like about this career? Position? Employer?

❑ What is your least favorite aspect?

❏ What do you do that is rewarding and satisfying for you?

❏ What background, training, and experience would best qualify me for this career and position?

❏ What aspects would be likely to cause burnout or frustration?

❏ What is an ordinary day and week like? Is it routine or always different?

❏ What personality characteristics are best suited to this work?

❏ Do people in this profession and company usually work overtime?

❏ What is the growth potential of this profession?

❏ Are there specific areas of the profession that are more in demand?

❏ Is this profession affected by rapidly changing technology?

❏ How much time and money are necessary to keep up with the changes?

❏ Would it be helpful to have a mentor?

❏ Is there an association for this profession where I can network and learn?

❏ Does the association provide mentors?

Ask Yourself Before an Interview

❏ Do I know enough about the job I am considering?

❏ How much do I know about the organization's history and achievements?

❏ Are my values congruent with the mission of this organization?

❏ What assumptions am I making about the job and organization that need to be clarified?

❏ Can I meet my personal and professional objectives in this job and in this organization?

❏ How do I best describe myself?

❑ What are my limitations? My strengths?

❑ If I were interviewing a candidate for this position what would I look for?

❑ Do my resume and cover letter reflect my education, relevant skills, achievements, and background?

Ask During the Interview

❑ What are the goals of this organization? What are its values?

❑ What is expected of me? Is there a detailed job description? Is it kept current? Are there responsibilities that aren't on the job description? How much time is spent on "other responsibilities as assigned"? Is the position responsible for informally training others?

❑ Are there clear policies and guidelines?

❑ Do I have the time, budget, knowledge, and support staff to meet the job objectives?

❑ How will I and the organization know that I have met expectations?

❑ How often are performance evaluations? Can I see performance criteria? Do employees have input into their performance evaluation? Are pay increases and promotional opportunities determined by the evaluation?

❑ What is the pay range for this job and how are increases determined? What has been the average pay increase? Do you expect the organization to continue granting pay increases?

❑ How much input do the employees have in policy making? Do they have opportunities to meet with or be part of decision-making teams?

❑ What are the career advancement opportunities in this position and organization? Is there potential for growth?

❑ What kind of orientation will I receive to the organization?

❑ What kind of training and education will I receive? Who will train me on my job? Who will answer my questions?

❑ What type of management style does top management use? What about my immediate manager?

❑ Who is my immediate supervisor? How often does the supervisor meet with people in the department?

❑ How are employees kept current on organizational projects, goals, and progress?

❑ Why did the person I am replacing leave this position? How long was the person here?

❑ What is the turnover rate of employees? What is the turnover rate in this position?

❑ Have there been lawsuits filed against this company by employees? If so, what kinds?

❑ Does the company have a cafeteria benefit selection program where employees pick and choose the coverage they want? What specific options and benefits are available?

❑ Does the company have on-site child care or any other type of offerings important to me?

❑ Are there educational and continuing education allowances?

❑ What criteria determine who gets educational stipends?

❑ Do you pay for any required association fees?

❑ Will I be able to attend conferences that are job related?

❑ Does the organization have employee networks?

DON'T FORGET

❑ Research upper management and the board of directors. Are women and minorities represented? (Current research indicates companies with diverse boards are more profitable.)

❑ Read the mission statement and employee manual carefully. Does the organization place a premium on valuing employees?

❏ Take note of the diversity level. Does the employee base represent a cross section of the population or is there a majority of one type, especially in upper management?

❏ Pay attention to red flags such as high rate of employee turnover, lack of older workers, management limited to one group.

❏ Observe the pictures on the walls and cartoons in the work areas.

❏ Listen carefully to people's language; do they make demeaning remarks or jokes?

❏ Research the organization's business dealings and reputation.

❏ Investigate whether they have had any lawsuits, the nature of the suits, and the outcomes.

Starting a
Business

A rt dreamed of starting a restaurant. He had verbal commitments from some investors to back the restaurant financially and to supply experienced staff. He leased a space. At the last minute the promise of money and staff fell through. Art found ways to borrow enough money to open, but he was seriously underfinanced and had a zero budget for advertising. Even though he had spent some time in the restaurant business he didn't know all the ins and outs of this very difficult industry. Eventually the business failed. *Lessons learned*: Get all promises in writing. Carefully research the business and the problems you may encounter. Develop an adequate advertising and marketing budget. Understand employee issues and have a back-up plan in case employees are late or absent. Don't start a business underfinanced. Find service-oriented employees for key positions.

Be very clear about why you want a business, the benefits of owning a business, what you need to sustain a business, and the background you and potential staff will need. Most people who thought running their own business would give them freedom have found that in many ways it is more demanding than working for someone else.

Ask Yourself

❑ Why do I want to have my own business? Am I clear about my goals and needs?

❑ What assumptions am I making about owning a small business?

❑ Are my personality, education, skills, and style conducive to owning and operating a small business? What are my strengths and weaknesses? Am I a self-starter? Do I like responsibility? Do I follow through? Am I self-disciplined? How well do I handle stress?

❑ Do I have the skills to be a manager—delegation, scheduling, counseling, and handling conflict?

❑ Am I willing to do every task that has to be done?

❑ Do I know enough about inventory control? Budgeting? Advertising? Payroll?

❑ What sacrifices am I willing to make? Giving up vacations? Working nights or weekends?

❑ What business and ethical values do I stand for? Are there environmental concerns I should think about? What about equal opportunity and affirmative action goals?

❑ Do I have a thorough knowledge of my product?

❑ How much of a salary or a draw do I need?

❑ Might I need to work at my old job part-time at first? Is this an option? Can I do that and still build a business?

❑ What will I need in terms of time and money to make me most productive?

❑ What kind of additional training may I need?

❑ Do I have the time for this business?

❑ What are my family needs and responsibilities? Do I see them changing in the near future?

❑ Would I like a partner to share costs and responsibilities? Do I need the expertise and skills of a partner? Can I find a partner with similar ethics and values?

❑ Do I want to buy an existing business or start my own?

❑ What will I need to start a business—business plan, money, supplies?

❑ Is there a need for this business?

❑ What do I need to do to demonstrate that this is a good business idea? What kind of research will confirm a need for this business? What will lenders want to see? Is there a specific format this lending institution requires for a business plan?

❑ Who will be my customers?

❑ Is there a specific location that needs this business? Is there a specific location that is better for this business?

❑ What kind of traffic pattern do I want or need?

❑ Are there zoning requirements that might affect my business?

❑ Am I aware of the changes and trends on the local, national, and international levels that may affect this business?

❑ Who is my competition? What do I have to offer that my competition doesn't? What does my competition have that I don't have?

❑ What type of a business adviser team, such as accountants and attorneys, will be beneficial?

❑ What are the regulations that will affect this business?

❑ What outside circumstances, such as weather, can influence my business?

❑ Are there associations for this business and profession that can provide me with help, support, and advice?

❑ Is there a business person that is willing to serve as a mentor?

❑ How much money do I need to start my business?

❑ What personal assets am I willing to put into this business?

❑ Do I need a loan? How is my credit history?

❑ How will I raise money? Do I want to involve friends, relatives, venture capitalists?

❑ Are there special loans for women, minority groups, for specific neighborhoods, or small businesses that I might qualify for?

❑ What is the minimum lease I can get? Are there escape clauses to allow for unforeseen circumstances? Is there a professional I should have review this lease?

❑ What kind of monthly budget will I need? What are my nonbusiness costs?

❑ Have I considered all costs: taxes, business supplies, equipment, advertising, merchandise, signage, parking, and utilities?

❑ What additional costs will I incur if I hire additional employees?

❑ What kind of business insurance do I need? Property and casualty? Liability? Errors and omissions or professional liability? Workmen's compensation? Disability? Health?

❑ What types of insurance costs do I need to pay at the state and federal levels for my employees?

❑ How much does it cost to have a business phone number? Will I be listed in the yellow pages?

❑ Do I want or need a special logo for my business cards and stationery? How much money do I need to spend on this?

❑ Will I need a business checking account? What is the cost? Will I need a business credit card?

❑ What kind of supplies and equipment will I need? Will used equipment be okay to start? Can I get some type of warranty on used equipment?

❑ What kind of cash flow will there be? Do I have enough reserve if the business doesn't meet my income expectations?

❑ What kinds of taxes will I need to pay?

❑ Do I need to collect sales tax? If so, do I have the necessary forms?

❑ What kind of credit can I establish with vendors? What will be the payment terms?

❑ Should this business be a sole proprietorship, partnership, or corporation? What are the legal and tax implications?

❑ How much will I need to charge to break even? To make a profit?

❑ What payment terms will I establish with my clients? Will I take credit cards? Offer discounts for cash payments? Bill them? Charge interest for late payments?

❑ Do I need a copyright or patent for my ideas?

❑ Do I need to register a name of the business? Do I register with the secretary of state or some other office?

❑ Have I checked with my state's department of commerce to see types of permits, licenses, and registrations I might need?

❑ What kinds of contracts do I need for this business?

❑ What types of written documents do I need? Do I need to file the documents?

❑ What hours will the business be open?

❑ What other employees will be needed? What education, training, and skill level should they have?

❑ Will I pay employees commission, straight salary, bonuses?

❑ What benefits do I want to offer? Am I willing to pay for hospitalization? Do I want to pay individual or family benefits? Will the employee need to contribute?

❑ What policies do I want to establish regarding vacation time: how many weeks, paid holidays, how many sick days, and how many years' service to get the time?

❑ Have I carefully thought through my values and expectations regarding customer service? How will I communicate them to my employees, vendors, and customers?

❑ How will I handle errors and dissatisfied or unhappy customers?

❑ How will I know if my customers and vendors are being treated the way I expect them to be treated?

❑ Do I have clear job descriptions and performance criteria?

❑ How often will I evaluate my employees?

❑ How will I provide training for my employees?

❑ How will I motivate my employees?

❑ What skills will I need to manage employees?

❑ What kind of ongoing communication system will I have to ensure information sharing and feedback? What type of system will I have to ensure that I hear from my employees and customers?

❑ Do I want some type of reward system for my employees? What do I want? How much do I want to spend?

Considering a Franchise

❑ Would I like to buy a franchise?

❑ What would it cost initially? Over time?

❑ What are franchisees in similar communities making?

❑ Have I visited with enough franchisers and asked enough question to make an intelligent decision about this business?

❑ Does the franchise have an expiration date? If so, what are the repurchase requirements?

❑ Can I choose the location of the franchise?

❑ Do I get territorial protection?

❑ Who are my direct, immediate competitors in this location? What kind of competition can I expect in the future?

❑ What services and training does the franchiser provide?

❑ Do they provide ongoing support?

❑ Do they provide advertising and customer leads?

❑ What rules would I have to follow?

❑ How much freedom would I have?

❑ Can I sell the business on my own?

❑ Must I make all purchases through the corporate offices?

Considering a Home-Based Business

❑ Do I have space for working at home? Is it large enough? Do I have enough storage space? Is it quiet enough? Am I out of the family traffic pattern?

❑ Am I disciplined enough to work at home?

❑ How will it affect my social life and family?

❑ What kind of equipment will I need?

❑ Will I need extra phone lines?

❑ Do I have adequate lighting and electrical wiring?

❑ Will clients be coming and going and might that be a problem in my neighborhood? Is there adequate parking?

❑ Do I need a separate entrance?

❑ Might clients feel uncomfortable walking through my home?

❑ Will I have a private phone number that only I or my employees will answer?

❑ Do I want to list my business in the yellow pages?

❑ What are the benefits and liabilities of being listed as a residence or business?

❑ Are there city or state regulations restricting business in my residential area?

❑ What types of licenses do I need? What types of permits are required?

DON'T FORGET

❑ Conduct thorough research on the business, location, trends, and environmental conditions that can affect the business you want to start.

❑ If going into a partnership, make sure all expectations and obligations are clear and contracted.

❑ Contact the small business administration, small business institutes, state department of trade, economic development or commerce, and secretary of state to get guidelines and information about starting a business, required permits, copyrights, patents, and hiring employees.

❑ Have a good team of advisers such as accountants and lawyers.

❑ Get a credit report on yourself to see how you are rated.

❑ Keep up-to-date on your competition as well as changes and advances in your field.

❑ Join associations or networks of people in your industry.

❑ Explore many marketing methods: local and targeted newspapers, door-to-door delivery, card deck mailings, computer networks, TV and radio advertising, giveaways, trade shows, catalogs, magazine advertisements, special events, opening-day celebrations, and so forth.

PART FOUR

From Generation to Generation

Hiring an In-Home Child-Care Provider

When I was pregnant with my first child, a friend gave me the name of a child-care provider who lived in my neighborhood. I was very fortunate because she had a flexible schedule that in turn gave me flexibility. She was quite strict and fastidious, which was different from my style. I was apprehensive about that, but my son seemed to like her. When my son was three-and-a-half years old, we took him on a trip leaving my infant daughter with the care provider. When we returned, the care provider proudly announced that she had weaned my daughter from the bottle. I thought it was too early to wean her and was quite unhappy that she had taken that liberty. I also was unhappy with myself because I had let the care provider exercise her ways over mine at times, and I hadn't aggressively looked for other care providers.

Lessons learned: Be clear about what you want and prioritize what is important to you. Be aware of philosophical, generational, cultural, and style differences about child rearing. Precisely communicate your needs, desires, and expectations. If the care provider tends to disregard your instructions, recognize it and decide whether her ways are acceptable.

Finding good, trustworthy care providers is challenging. A referral from someone whose values, discipline, and lifestyle are similar to yours is probably the best source. In addition, your community might have resources to locate skilled care providers. Check to see if there are Red Cross or other types of child-care certification courses offered through community centers, hospitals, or schools. Additional resources are colleges or nursing schools, religious institutions, child-care resource centers or referral services, and senior citizen groups. When meeting with potential care providers, ask yourself if this person will set a good example for your children by language, behavior, grooming, patience and common sense.

Ask Yourself

❑ Does my child have any special needs or preferences?

❑ How many and what hours will the care provider work? Would there be additional times I will need someone?

❑ What are my expectations of care providers? Clean the house? Cook meals? Chauffeur the children? Entertain the children? Put toys away? Put children to sleep?

❑ Does the salary I am willing to pay reflect the importance and responsibilities of the job?

❑ What are the guidelines I expect a care provider to follow — language used, behavior, phone and television privileges, visits by children's friends or care provider's friends, stay awake after the children go to sleep, how phone is answered, smoking privileges?

Ask the Child-Care Provider

❑ Have you had any special training such as a baby-sitting course or CPR?

❑ What are your experiences with children?

❑ Do you have siblings you have had to care for (if the care provider is young)?

❑ What are your child-rearing philosophies (if the care provider is an adult)?

❑ Why do you like to take care of children?

❑ What are your favorite and least favorite aspects of taking care of children?

❑ What behavior limits do you set with a child? What would you do if a child misbehaves? Doesn't pay attention to you? Won't go to sleep?

❑ How would you console an unhappy child?

❑ Do you believe physical discipline is acceptable in any circumstances? (Probe answer.)

❑ What are your beliefs about physical contact such as hugging or holding the child?

❑ Do you like to play with children? What kind of play? What kinds of activities would you do with my child? What kinds of toys would you view as acceptable for this child?

❑ Do you do the things I need such as clean or drive?

❑ How long have you had a driver's license? What is your driving record? Any accidents or speeding tickets?

❑ Do you presently take any medications? Smoke? Do you have any type of drinking or drug problem? Have you in the past?

❑ What are your special interests and hobbies?

❑ What TV shows do you watch regularly?

❑ Have you had other jobs where you had the same duties you will have here?

❑ Do you mind sitting if my child is ill?

❑ Can you provide me with references?

❑ When are you available?

❑ How far in advance do I need to call you?

❑ What do you charge?

DON'T FORGET

❑ In addition to work references ask for the name of a teacher or someone who can vouch for the person's character.

❑ Before you hire a new person, invite him to your home for a tour, to familiarize the child with the care provider, and to watch how the care provider and child interact.

❑ Decide with the care provider what your children should call him.

❑ If you hire a live-in person, set very clear boundaries about responsibilities, hours, expectations about discipline, free time, acceptable television programs, and so on.

❑ If your child has certain tendencies, behavior problems, or physical problems be honest about them and tell the care provider how you want her to handle those incidents.

❑ Put important rules in writing and go over them: the house address and phone number, care provider's privileges, eating hours and acceptable food, sleep time and sleep arrangements, discipline, medicines to take, allowable TV, special needs, how to answer the phone, emergency procedures and where you can be reached, and where things are located.

❑ Let the care provider know if there might be unexpected visitors, what to do if any visitors or family members come by, and whether children may leave with anyone.

❑ If you are concerned about privacy, tell the care provider that what goes on in your home stays there.

❑ Tell the care provider who will be taking her home and when. Make sure you do not send the care provider home with someone who has been drinking.

Selecting Day-Care Centers or Nursery Schools

When many of my friends were selecting nursery schools, I was completing my bachelor's degree. I was considering teaching at a nursery school and visited several of them. At that time one particular school was very popular. It was quite a distance for some of my friends and more expensive than some of the others but it was *the* school to go to. As I looked around the facilities of this school, I couldn't see a difference that would warrant the added expense or longer traveling time. I mentioned this to some of my friends who automatically were sending their children without looking at the other schools. Some then investigated and sent their children to different schools. *Lessons learned*: Don't jump on a bandwagon without checking out options. The reasons one person might like a school or day-care center may not necessarily apply to you or your child. Observe teachers and staff and request those you think would work most effectively with your child.

Ask Yourself

❑ Does my child have special needs to consider?

❑ Do I have work times or needs that might affect my choices?

❑ Do I need any financial subsidies?

❑ What kind of environment do I want my child to be in—family environment, a home or facility, grouped by age or mixed ages, educational emphasis, small group, large group? Do I want a religious environment?

❑ What are my priorities? Is location important? Cost? Flexibility in drop-off and pickup times?

❑ What are my values about discipline? Affection? Structure?

❑ What are my expectations of the staff?

❑ Will the staff set good examples for my children by their behavior, language, and grooming?

Ask the Facility

❑ How long have you been in business?

❑ Is this facility state certified?

❑ When was the last time the board of health or building inspectors examined the facility? Have you passed all your inspections? Have you ever been in violation?

❑ Is the facility childproof (no exposed radiators, sharp edges, cupboards and doors easily opened, medicines or other dangerous products reachable)?

❑ Are you well equipped for all ages?

❑ How many cribs and playpens do you have? How many children may be in a playpen at one time? How long do you leave the children in playpens?

❑ Do you keep the facility secured?

❑ Is the facility air conditioned?

❑ What is the temperature setting in the winter? Spring? Summer? Fall?

❑ Does the facility close for holidays? Are you willing to take children on holidays? Weekends? Overnight?

❑ Do you provide meals? Where is the food cooked and stored? What are some typical menus? Will you prepare foods for special dietary requirements? What accommodations do you make if a child doesn't like the food you prepare? What kinds of snacks do you provide? How often during the day are snacks given? Are the children supervised when they eat?

❑ Do you administer medication? Do I need to provide you with a note? Would you give my child any medication, such as aspirin, without consulting me? Where do you store medications?

❑ Where do you change diapers? How do you sanitize the changing area?

❑ Do you allow parents to drop off children without a reservation? If so, how do you ensure that the staff-child ratio is met?

❑ Are you willing to provide me with references?

Ask About Staff

❑ What is the ratio of certified early childhood teachers and support staff to children?

❑ What are the care providers' credentials? How have they been trained? Where did they receive their training?

❑ How thoroughly have you checked references and other background information?

❑ Do you check criminal records?

❑ What criteria are used in hiring the staff?

❑ What are the strengths of your staff?

❑ Are the staff trained in CPR? First aid? Emergency procedures for fires, storms, or tornadoes? Do they know what to do if an unknown person comes to pick up a child? What are the policies and procedures?

❑ Are the staff required to stay current on child-care issues? What kind of continuing education must they complete?

❑ What is the staff turnover rate from year to year? How many are new this year?

❑ How long have the staff my child will come in contact with worked at this facility?

❑ Who manages the staff on site?

❑ How are they held accountable for their jobs? What performance criteria are used to determine if they are good with the children? If they adequately follow policies?

❑ What kind of support is available to the staff if they are having problems with a child—staff meetings, psychologists, social workers?

❑ How often do staff take breaks? Who replaces them? If someone has to leave for an emergency or is ill do you operate short-staffed? Do you have substitutes available?

Ask About Philosophy

❑ Are parents welcome to drop in?

❑ How do you formally and informally communicate about activities? News items? Child's progress?

❑ What are the goals and objectives of the program?

❑ What can I do at home to foster your goals?

❑ Do you encourage parent involvement at this facility? If there is a problem with a child, at what point do you talk with the parents? Are parents used as volunteers for field trips and facility programming?

❑ How do you cultivate positive interaction among the children?

❑ Do you accept sick children? How long should my child be without symptoms before she returns to the facility?

❑ What are the procedures if a child gets sick or injured while at the facility?

❑ How do you take care of sick children to assure that other children aren't exposed?

❑ What are your standards about weaning and toilet training? Do you discuss these standards with parents as to when and how?

❑ What happens if I am delayed in picking up my child?

❑ What is the discipline policy? Do all the staff agree to adhere to this policy?

❑ What is the hugging policy?

❑ How often are babies held?

❑ What do you do with an unhappy or ornery child?

❑ How do you ensure that the child does not leave the facility with an unauthorized person?

Ask About Programming

❑ What kind of learning activities are offered? May I see the daily schedule?

❑ Does the facility provide multicultural, gender-fair programming and environment?

❑ Is there any type of religious programming? What is it? Do you celebrate specific holidays? Are you willing to meet the needs of other groups?

❑ How do you ensure that the child uses age-appropriate toys? Do you keep the babies apart from children who may play with games and toys that could be dangerous to an infant?

❑ What type of physical exercise do the children get? How often?

❑ What kind of art and music activities do they do?

❑ How often do the children watch TV? Videos? What do they watch?

❑ How often do the children go outside? Where do they go? How are they supervised?

❑ Do you take the children on outings or field trips? Where to? Who drives? Do you check the driving records (accidents, tickets) of the people who provide transportation on these outings? Do you have enough car seats for all the children? If a bus is used, are there safety belts for the children?

Ask About Demographics

❑ What is the maximum number of children you accept?

❑ How many children of each age bracket do you accept?

❑ What criteria do you use to group children?

❑ Do the children come from culturally diverse backgrounds?

❑ What's the average length of time that a child remains at this facility?

Ask About Cost

❑ What is the cost of the program?

❑ Are there subsidies available?

❑ Do I have to pay if my child is sick or on vacation?

❑ What is included in the cost?

❑ Will there be extra charges? What are they?

❑ Can I get child-care credit on my income tax return?

DON'T FORGET

❑ Since some facilities have a long waiting list, you might need to look before your baby is born.

❑ Call your state department of human services and your county to find licensed providers. Also check to see whether places you are considering have ever had a license revoked or been denied a license.

❑ Check with your state board of health to determine whether places you are considering have been in violation and whether they have passed all inspections.

❑ Get referrals from people you trust.

❑ Observe activities in the facility (more than once).

❑ Find out about staff turnover. A high rate may be a red flag as to the true operation of the facility.

❑ Get to know the staff. Do they seem warm, supportive, and friendly?

❑ Observe teachers and staff and request those you think would work most effectively with your child.

❑ Make sure the equipment is clean and in good working condition.

❑ Inspect the facility to determine the cleanliness of the bathrooms, food preparation areas, diaper changing areas, and play areas.

❑ Observe other children to see if they seem happy, content, and clean.

❑ Make certain that the environment is cheery.

❑ Assess the visuals in the rooms to see what lessons they are portraying.

❑ Talk to other parents about their experiences.

❑ Trust your gut if you have a bad feeling.

❑ If your child came along when you visited the facility, ask what she thought about it.

❑ Drop in unexpectedly to make sure the facility is run as you have been told.

❑ Once you have selected a facility, keep watching and listening to ensure that your expectations are being met. Are they changing their visuals? What kind of lessons are they teaching your children?

❑ If your child tells you stories about the facility, take him seriously. Watch for any behavior changes. If your child seems reluctant to go to the facility, probe for the reason. Don't discount what your child relates.

❑ Establish a code word with the facility that would allow someone else to pick up your child in case of an emergency.

Selecting a
Children's Camp

In June 1989, my thirteen-year-old daughter incurred injuries when a tornado swept through her camp. Much to my surprise, I learned that the children and counselors had not practiced fire or tornado drills. In fact they didn't even have a comprehensive procedure. It occurred to me, after my daughter's accident, that when I served as a camp recruiter, not one family in three years had asked me about emergency procedures or counselor training. I realized that I had assumed that if schools that have children for just eight hours a day are required to take children through emergency procedures, a camp that has our children for twenty-four hours a day would certainly have to do the same. *Lessons learned*: Clarify assumptions. Don't take anything for granted. Safety is a big concern and should be addressed.

In selecting a camp for your child, you want to make sure the camp program is of interest to your child, that there are clear guidelines and procedures governing the camp, that there is accountability in the system, that counselors are well trained, and that campers are taken through emergency procedures.

Although the questions that follow are geared for overnight camps, most of them could and should be asked of day camps, too.

Ask Yourself and the Camper

❑ Does the child have special needs we should consider in selecting a camp?

❑ What activities are important?

❑ What other camp criteria are important to us—day or overnight, location and distance, length and dates of sessions, demographics of the campers, transportation to and from camp, quality of the staff, religious affiliation?

❑ Is the camper ready to attend overnight camp?

❑ Would the camper prefer to go with a friend?

Ask the Facility

❑ What are the staff's credentials? How old are staff members? What are their backgrounds?

❑ What is the camper-staff ratio?

❑ What kind of training do counselors receive? What qualifications do the trainers have?

❑ What percentage of the staff return each year?

❑ What type of health facilities are there? How many beds are there for sick or injured campers?

❑ Do you use skilled specialists for any of the activities?

❑ If the campers have free time, who supervises them during this time?

❑ Who is with the campers on the counselor's day off?

❑ Do the counselors stay in the cabins after the campers are asleep?

❑ What do you do to ensure that counselors are not bringing alcohol or drugs into the camp?

❑ What is the distance from my child's cabin to the dining room, sports facilities, infirmary, and the main office?

❑ What sports facilities do you have: tennis, water skiing, swimming, archery, horseback riding, canoeing, sailing, golfing?

❑ What do you do for the children if there is extreme heat or incessant rain?

❑ What are your policies regarding sexual relationships among campers? Among counselors? Between campers and counselors? How do you enforce the policies?

Ask About Health and Emergency Procedures

❑ Do you call parents if there is an injury or illness? How serious does it need to be before you contact the parent? How soon do you call after the injury or illness?

❑ What precautions do you take if there is a communicable disease?

❑ Under what circumstances do campers stay in the infirmary?

❑ Are the campers rehearsed in emergency procedures? Do the emergency procedures encompass all types of emergencies: tornadoes, hurricanes, floods, severe thunderstorms, fires, severe heat, fighting or rioting among campers, waterfront safety, and physical problems like a diabetic reaction, measles, or injuries?

❑ Are there first aid stations throughout the camp?

❑ Are rules and procedures posted around camp?

❑ Is the medical staff available twenty-four hours a day?

❑ How close is the nearest hospital?

❑ If a camper has to go to the hospital in an ambulance does a staff person go along? Does a staff person stay with the camper through medical procedures? How quickly do you contact a parent?

❑ What kind of insurance coverage does the camp have if a camper is injured? If property is stolen or damaged?

Ask About Programming

❑ What kind of orientation are the children given when they arrive at camp?

❑ How much time will the children spend at the activities that interest them: horseback riding, water skiing, sailing, swimming, theater, arts and crafts?

❑ Are they guaranteed to get the activities that are attracting them to this camp?

❑ Is there any type of religious programming? What kind and how often?

❑ How much free time is there? Is it supervised? Are the campers allowed to leave the camp by themselves, with other campers, and how often?

❑ What activities are available during free time?

❑ Are there any activities away from the grounds?

❑ What is done about homesick and lonely children?

❑ How flexible are you in hearing and meeting campers' individual needs like adjustment problems, bed wetting, shyness, adjustments to stress?

❑ Do you facilitate friendships among children?

❑ Do you make provisions for special diets and fussy eaters?

❑ Do you require the children to write home? How often?

Ask About Demographics

❑ How many campers are the same age and gender as my child?

❑ How are the children grouped?

❑ How many campers to a cabin?

❑ Do the children come from culturally diverse backgrounds?

Ask About Costs

❑ How much does this camp cost? Are there discounts for campers who attend multiple sessions? For families with multiple campers?

❑ What does the cost include?

❑ Are there any extra fees?

❏ What can campers buy on the grounds?

❏ Does the camp manage the campers' money?

❏ Do you let the campers know the status of their funds?

❏ How much pocket money do the campers need? (Check this with previous campers also.)

❏ Is there a money-back policy if a child is miserable at camp and returns home?

DON'T FORGET

❏ Talk to past campers and counselors about the camp.

❏ Try to find out how many campers and counselors return from previous years. This may be an indication of the camp's success.

❏ Call the American Camping Association (317–342–8456) to find out if the camp is accredited. Find out how this camp rated on its last review and what criteria ACA used in this process. Ask if there were any criteria this camp failed to meet.

❏ Call the Better Business Bureau, the state attorney general's office, and the board of health to see whether there have been any complaints against the camp or licenses revoked or denied.

❏ Ask your child to write to you about the orientation and about other concerns you may have.

Selecting a College

There could be a hundred different names in this story because I have heard it so many times. Over the years many students have told me they were surprised to encounter difficulty getting into the college courses they needed to graduate. This has kept many students from graduating on time. While it is more common at larger universities, it happens everywhere. I know of one student at a small liberal arts college who needed only one more course to graduate. The problem was that this course was offered only in the spring. The college would not accept the credit if he took the course elsewhere, so he stayed home fall semester and went back the following spring. For this one course, his parents had to pay an entire semester's worth of fees. Several years ago I had the same problem. I needed the last quarter of a statistics course to graduate and it wasn't offered that year. Fortunately, my college created a work experience for me to get the credits. *Lessons learned*: Don't make assumptions. Ask the average graduation time, the ease of getting into required courses and specific fields. Are there alternatives to taking classes at the school such as independent study or work experience? Will the college accept credits from other schools?

Colleges and universities come in all shapes and sizes, in various locations, and with different philosophies. They market themselves with impressive informational brochures and on-campus tours. When selecting a college, the physical environment may be important, but primarily you want to gain an understanding of the day-to-day functioning of the school and whether it is the best place for the prospective student.

I had the opportunity to be the parent orientation coordinator at the University of Minnesota the year before my son was going to start his college selection process. After hearing the concerns of more than 1,200 parents, I learned a lot of questions to ask. Even so, I still didn't anticipate all my concerns.

Ask Yourself (Parents)

❑ What type of learning environment is best for my young adult?

❑ What do we consider the most important criteria—the type of institution, programs offered, distance, class size, size of the school, demographics, liberal arts, a research environment, the professors' qualifications, job placement assistance?

❑ Are we in agreement about what our student wants and needs?

❑ Would our student learn better with small classes or are large classes okay?

❑ Do we want the student close to home?

❑ Will every family member be comfortable seeing each other infrequently?

❑ How much money are we willing to spend on a college education?

❑ Do we want our child to take out student loans?

❑ Do we qualify for federal financial aid? Does my child's high school have computer software to help us determine whether we meet federal criteria? Do local colleges or high schools have financial aid nights I can attend to learn more about obtaining federal funding? What if we are not willing to contribute to our child's education, do we still have to report our income?

❏ Are the colleges our child is considering well endowed? How many scholarships did they give last year? What is the average amount of a scholarship? Do they grant full scholarships? What are the requirements to obtain scholarships? Do the colleges have financial aid officers we can speak with?

❏ Do we want our child to look for colleges that may give scholarships for special talents and achievements?

❏ How much money are we willing to spend on traveling costs and long-distance phone bills?

❏ Can we afford for the student to join a sorority, fraternity, or social club?

❏ How much time do we expect the student to take to obtain a degree?

❏ Will we allow the student to select a major of her choice?

Ask Yourself (Students)

❏ Do I want a liberal arts education or specific career preparation? Do I want to consider community or technical colleges, private schools, or public universities? What are the benefits of each option?

❏ What academic and career interests do I have?

❏ What special skills, experience, and academic record do I need to get into my various choices?

❏ Am I free to select the major of my choice? Do the colleges I am considering offer my major? Do they excel in that area?

❏ What type of community do I want the institution to be based in: size of town, demographics, cultural offerings, distance to other colleges, cities, and events?

❏ What expectations do I have of a college environment: do I want an active Greek system, a commuter campus, a campus where all the social life takes place on campus, where students stay on campus all weekend?

❏ Do I prefer small or large class sizes?

❑ Would I prefer a small or large college?

❑ What type of activities do I want to be involved in: sports, social, volunteer, religious?

❑ Do I want to be close to home?

❑ Will I be comfortable far away from my family and friends?

❑ Am I friends with anyone else who attends this school? Will I be comfortable going to college without any friends from home?

❑ Will I need to work at a job if I attend a specific college? Can I work and still give enough attention to my studies?

❑ If I need to take out student loans, am I comfortable with the obligations I will incur?

❑ How much time do I expect to take to obtain a degree?

❑ What type of living arrangement would I like?

❑ Am I in agreement with my parents over these issues?

Ask the College About Demographics

❑ What is the typical profile of a student: gender, academic background, racial and cultural background, geographic location?

❑ What percentage of the freshman students graduate? Drop out?

❑ What percentage of students transfer to other schools?

❑ If it is a two-year college, what percentage of the students go on to four-year colleges? If a technical college, do students get credits or a degree that will be accepted by other colleges? What percentage of students who apply to four-year colleges get in? What four-year colleges does the school have relationships with?

Ask the College About Admission Procedures

❑ What are admission requirements?

❑ Do you have a rolling admission in which students can apply and be accepted any time?

❑ Do you have early action or early decision admissions? Is there a benefit to applying early? Is there an obligation if the student is accepted early?

❑ Is the admission process blind to need, race, and gender? Is there a minority ratio?

❑ What are the application deadlines?

❑ Is it beneficial to have an interview either on or off campus by staff, alumni, or both?

❑ How important is the student's academic record?

❑ What college entrance exams do you accept? What weight is given to them?

❑ How important are past extracurricular activities as a qualification for admission?

❑ What can the student do to maximize her chances of admission?

❑ What percentage of the students are transfer students?

❑ How can the student show commitment to the college before admission? For example, is it an advantage to tell you if this is her first choice?

Ask the College About Philosophy and Programming

❑ Is this a liberal arts or career preparation institute? How many majors are offered? Are there any interdisciplinary majors available?

❑ Does the institution stress research or teaching for the faculty?

❑ What percentage of introductory courses are taught by graduate students?

❑ What percentage of the classes over the four years of enrollment will be taught by teaching assistants?

❑ Are teaching assistants required to complete a teaching seminar?

❏ What are the class sizes in typical introductory courses such as English, economics, political science, or psychology?

❏ When does a student need to declare a major?

❏ Are students guaranteed to get the major of their choice?

❏ What is the average length of time it takes for a student to obtain a degree?

❏ Are there any common course requirements that all students must take before they graduate?

❏ Are any fields or courses more difficult to get into?

❏ How do students register for courses?

❏ Can students usually get the courses they need in a given semester or quarter? What happens if they can't?

❏ What is the average size of classes?

❏ Are the classes mainly lecture, discussion, or both?

❏ What are the credentials of the faculty?

❏ Do the faculty strive to offer equal opportunities to students regardless of gender, race, or cultural background? What kind of awareness and training have they had to sensitize themselves to differences? To different learning styles?

❏ Are there tutorial options if the student wants or needs help with course work or writing papers?

❏ What percentage of your students go on to graduate school?

❏ Do you offer any graduate programs?

❏ Do you have any relationships with other schools that make it easier for your graduates to get accepted to graduate programs?

❏ Do you have a parent orientation program? A first-year student orientation program? A dorm orientation program?

❏ How many trips does the student have to make to campus before the semester begins for orientations, testing, and dorm assignments?

❏ Do you communicate to parents during the year?

❑ Do you sponsor social events to help students meet?

❑ Do you have resident advisers who help students become acclimated? To meet other students? Who are the resident advisers? What criteria are used to select them? What are their responsibilities?

❑ What specific dates do we need to know about?

❑ Does the college help students find work during their student years? Are there many on-campus jobs available? Are the on-campus jobs available only for students who have received financial aid? How difficult is it for the student to find work?

❑ Do you have career, academic, psychological, or personal counseling available? Are there any fees for these services?

❑ Does the school or faculty have job connections in specific areas?

❑ What kinds of personal-growth courses or support systems are available?

❑ Does the school plan programming, courses, and research around current and projected trends in the workplace and society?

Ask the College About Student Lifestyles

❑ Are the students allowed to stay at school during holidays?

❑ Do most students stay on campus over weekends? If not, where do they go?

❑ Does the school provide transportation to the airports or train stations? What outside transportation services are there? How often are they available? How does the student make arrangements for these services?

❑ Are the students allowed to have cars? If so, what is the parking availability for cars? Are there any parking fees?

❑ What percentage of the students have cars?

❑ How active is the Greek system? What percentage of the student body belongs to fraternities or sororities? Are people who don't belong to the Greek system welcome at their parties and other social events?

❑ Are there certain groups (political, sexual preference, racial, cultural) that influence the campus environment?

❑ What religious institutions or groups are on campus? How active are they? Are they also connected with off-campus groups?

❑ What kinds of social, academic, physical, extracurricular activities are available? Are they available to all students? What are the qualifications? Any extra fees?

❑ What kind of causes do the students get involved with?

❑ What is the school's relationship with the surrounding community?

❑ What kind of physical education facilities are available?

❑ What kind of health services do you have? Are the services available twenty-four hours a day?

❑ Have there been hate crimes or other types of disturbing incidents on campus? When was the last problem? How have you resolved these types of problems?

❑ What is the availability of computers on campus? Is there a computer network on campus used by the faculty and students? Are there benefits for a student to bring her own computer? What kind?

Ask the College About Housing

❑ What kind of housing facilities do you have? Are there special-interest living quarters based on language, sports, or other interests?

❑ What is the deadline to sign up for housing? Is there a benefit to getting the application in early?

❑ Are all furnishings provided? Are students allowed to alter the rooms? Can they paint their rooms?

❑ Is some housing more difficult to get?

❑ Can students request a specific dormitory? What's the likelihood this request will be honored?

❑ Is housing guaranteed for four years?

❑ What percentage of the rooms are single rooms?

❑ Are there certain dorms for freshmen? For other academic years?

❑ Are there coed facilities? Are there men-only and women-only facilities or floors? Are there shared bathrooms?

❑ Is there a cleaning service for common areas? Students' rooms? How often are the common areas cleaned? The students' rooms?

❑ Can the students have microwaves in the dorms? Do they need or can they have other cooking equipment?

❑ Are all the living quarters equipped with fire alarms? How often are they checked? Do you have fire drills?

❑ How do you match roommates for first-year students?

❑ What if the roommates don't get along?

❑ Are students allowed to live off campus? What types of off-campus housing are available? How easy is it to find off-campus housing?

Ask the College About Costs

❑ Do you have (and do we need) tuition reimbursement insurance in case the student drops out?

❑ If cost is determined by credit, can the student get money back if she drops a course by a certain time? What are the policies regarding reimbursement?

❑ Are there special scholarships or funding the student qualifies for? Do you assist in obtaining that funding?

❑ Are there extra fees for using any of the facilities or services?

❑ How many and which meals are included in the meal plan? How much more money does the typical student spend on food?

❑ What extra costs will there be (such as laboratory or field trips)?

❑ What does the typical student spend on course books and other materials per year?

❑ Is health insurance included in the fees?

❑ Is the student's property insured or do we need additional insurance?

❑ If the student is granted aid the first year, is it guaranteed for all four years?

❑ How difficult is it for students to get jobs off or on campus?

Ask the College About Safety

❑ What kind of crime has occurred on campus in the last year?

❑ Has there been an increase in certain types of crime?

❑ Is theft a problem on campus, specifically in dorms, libraries, classrooms, or eating facilities?

❑ Are the majority of crimes committed by students or off-campus residents?

❑ What kinds of precautions are taken by the college to decrease crime?

❑ Is the campus well lit?

❑ Are there campus safety personnel? Are they licensed peace officers? What kind of relationship does campus safety personnel have with campus police? With community police?

❑ Is there a certain type of bike lock that is recommended?

❑ Is there an escort service or other safety resources after dark?

❑ Is there a safety unit in student orientation? What subjects does it cover (date rape, walking alone, personal property theft)?

❑ Is there a rape counseling center that provides information and counseling?

DON'T FORGET

❑ Read resource books that describe colleges such as *Princeton Big Book of Colleges, Barron's Profiles of American Colleges, Inside Look at America's Best Colleges*, and *The Insiders' Guide to Colleges*; there are many of them and they address many, varied issues.

❑ Talk to a college counselor. There are private consultants available if your school does not provide adequate service.

❑ Try to locate people from your area who have attended or have students at the college and talk with them. The school may be able to put you in contact with present or previous students.

❑ Attend college fairs to meet representatives from the schools.

❑ Check with your high school to see if they have videos of the colleges you are considering.

❑ Find out when college representatives may be visiting high schools in your area.

❑ Take tours of the colleges.

❑ Arrange for your student to spend the night on campus to meet other students and see how they live.

❑ Sit in on classes.

❑ Attend social events.

❑ Walk around campus and look at posters, bulletins, and students.

❑ Read the college's student newspaper.

Selecting
Short- or Long-Term
Health Care

I was at a friend's house for dinner one night when her ninety-year-old mother-in-law called, anxious and scared. Her new home health care provider had just arrived—a young woman with green hair and two nose rings. My friend managed to calm her mother-in-law. She pointed out that even though her appearance was unusual, the caregiver might be a very nice person. She suggested her mother-in-law try talking to her. Within a few minutes the phone rang again. By now the patient was semihysterical. My friend's husband went to his mother's house to defuse the situation. At first he was skeptical; the caregiver was dressed inappropriately and chewing gum. After talking with her a while, he discovered a scared, inexperienced person who wanted to do a good job. He decided she would be fine for the evening and eventually got his mother to agree.

Lessons learned: Make the patient's needs and preferences known to the agency. Find out the agency's employee screening methods and rules for caregivers. If possible, arrange for the patient to meet the caregiver beforehand, or have someone he trusts with him when the caregiver arrives.

Kathryn has worked as an aide in a long-term care center for twelve years; she is a caring, dedicated employee. Her observations reinforce my own experience working in a long-term care facility. In the facility where I worked, the floor reserved for people receiving the most intensive care was referred to with demeaning names. Even worse, so were the residents. This is painful for the family. It is difficult to watch someone who has been doing relatively well go downhill; it is even more difficult when this means moving to a floor that is notorious. Yet such moves are not uncommon. It is also common, according to Kathryn, for residents and their families to disagree with the care facility's assessment of the resident's health. *Lessons learned*: Look at the whole facility and pay attention to the surroundings. Circumstances can change, and the resident may not be living in the environment you first select. If you don't agree with the evaluation of the patient, get a second opinion.

Hospital stays, home health care, hospice care, assisted-living facilities, nursing homes—with so many options for both short- and long-term care, it can be difficult to select a facility that provides the level of care you need at a price you can afford. Remember that there might be free or low-cost resources available from your community. Before making any decisions, assess your needs and resources, consult the patient (if other than yourself), and then learn as much as you can about available options so you can make an informed decision.

In the Beginning, Ask Yourself

❑ What are the present personal and physical needs of the person who needs care?

❑ Based on his present condition, what are the expectations about his future health needs?

❑ What resources—family members and friends, time others can spend, and money—are available to him?

❑ Does he like to be with other people rarely, frequently, most of the time?

❑ What fears and stereotypes do we need to address to make the best decision?

❏ Do we know people who have faced a similar situation who can suggest good people or recommend care facilities?

❏ Do we need to consider assigning power of attorney or appointing a conservator to handle financial matters?

Selecting Home Health Care

One available option is home health care, which allows people with a chronic illness or during recuperation to stay in their own home. The Department of Labor lists it as the fastest-growing section of health care. The field has grown so rapidly that by 1992, 82 percent of all accredited medical schools offered home health care courses.

Ask Yourself

❏ Is home health care the best option for this person?

❏ How much care does he need? Does he need personal services such as cooking, feeding, bathing, and getting dressed? Does he need medical procedures such as shots or checkups? Does he need a companion?

❏ How long will he need someone, either temporarily or full time?

❏ How many hours a day?

❏ Does he need help during sleeping hours?

❏ Are there family members or friends who are willing to take care of the patient?

❏ Is the home safe for the patient? Can he reach everyday supplies? Can he open medicine and administer it himself?

❏ Is he able to care for himself if a health care provider doesn't come?

❏ Is he mentally alert enough to call for help? Is the phone easily accessible? Are emergency numbers in a convenient location?

❑ Might he wander?

❑ Does he know what to do in case of a tornado, fire, or other emergency?

❑ Are written instructions available for the care provider?

❑ Should we invest in medical emergency systems or security systems that make it easy for the patient to call for help?

❑ How difficult, resistant, or critical is the patient? Might we need to coach a care provider on idiosyncrasies and how to best get along with him?

❑ What kind of supplies or devices might he need or desire?

Ask About Community Resources

❑ What options and services are available in the community?

❑ If needed, are there subsidized options?

❑ Is there a Meals On Wheels program in the community?

❑ Do any social service agencies help with home care?

❑ Are there vans that come to the home or other resources that will enable the patient to have lab tests and medical procedures performed at home?

❑ Are there social service agencies with volunteers to drive a patient to the hospital or make home visits?

❑ Are there local day-care programs that provide care and activities? What kinds of services are offered (meals, various therapies, medication, tests)? What kinds of programs are provided (discussion groups, crafts, entertainment)? Is transportation available? Are family members welcome to drop in or attend programs?

Ask If You Are Hiring Health Care Providers Yourself

❑ Why do you want to do this work?

❑ What is your work experience?

❑ Have you bathed a patient before? Cooked? Administered medication? Performed any other service the patient needs?

❑ Have you handled someone with similar problems? What types of situations have you encountered?

❑ How do you manage conflict and disagreement?

❑ What types of people do you have a hard time getting along with? How do you handle difficult people?

❑ Are you strong enough to help if the patient falls?

❑ Do you have a car and can you take the patient to appointments?

❑ How much do you charge?

❑ Do you have other jobs or a life situation that may interfere with your coming each day?

Ask If You Are Selecting an Agency

❑ Are you a certified Medicare agency?

❑ How large a staff do you have?

❑ Do you have physical therapists? Speech therapists? (Others as needed?) Can you run any tests the patient may need? If not, do you make arrangements or help locate the proper resources?

❑ What is the employee turnover rate?

❑ What kind of prescreening and background checks do you do on your employees? Do you do criminal checks? Do you hire people with criminal backgrounds?

❑ How do you ensure employees' skills are adequate?

❑ What standards and criteria, such as dress code, do you set for employees?

❑ Do you have an orientation and ongoing training for your employees?

❑ Do you assess the patient to determine her needs and assign employees that best meet them?

❑ Are we assured of always having our home health care needs met by your agency? What percentage of the time are you unable to meet a client's needs?

❑ Can we request the gender of the employee who will bathe and tend the patient?

❑ Can we get employees with different skill levels for different hours of the day?

❑ How long has the person you are sending been doing home health care?

❑ What is her training? Are her experience and training sufficient to meet the needs of the patient?

❑ Will the person clean the house? Cook?

❑ Does she drive and can she take the patient to appointments?

❑ Can we get the same person every day?

❑ What kind of facilities are we required to have for overnight help?

❑ Are you bonded? Do you cover the cost if things are missing or damaged?

About Finances

❑ What is the fee structure? Is there a minimum number of hours we need to employ help?

❑ Does the patient have long-term care coverage that includes home health care?

❑ Does the patient have any other insurance that covers home health care?

❑ Will Medicare cover home health care for this situation?

❑ Do you have to be hospitalized first to receive payment?

❑ Does the doctor have to prescribe home health care for it to be covered?

❑ Is there a maximum time the reimbursement will cover?

❑ Is there a deductible?

❏ How often do you bill?

❏ Will the agency complete and submit all necessary insurance paperwork?

Hospice Care for Patients with Life-Limiting Illnesses

People who have a life-limiting illness need special care. Hospice care is designed to meet the comfort needs these people require. Hospice care can be given at a person's home or in a facility especially designed for these patients.

Ask the Facility

❏ Is the patient a candidate for a hospice program?

❏ Are residential and home care hospice services available? Is there a limit to how much care the patient can receive at home?

❏ How would the family and the patient benefit from a hospice program?

❏ If the patient needs extensive care will he be able to get into a residential hospice or long-term care facility?

❏ Can the patient receive treatment through a hospice program? If he goes into remission can he still receive hospice care?

❏ Do you [the hospice facility or agency] continually reassess the needs of the family and patient?

❏ Will you train family members in caregiving?

❏ Do you have volunteers who will sit with the patient?

❏ What kinds of services are available for family members during and after the illness? Do you provide counseling for the patient and family members?

❏ What services are provided? Do you offer a range of therapies such as art, music, massage, and speech?

❏ Do you have or can you recommend support groups?

About Finances

❑ What is the fee structure?

❑ Does the community offer a hospice facility to residents in need of care? Are subsidies available? Does the subsidy offered by the community cover care only in a particular facility or can it be applied to any local facility?

❑ Is hospice care covered by the patient's insurance? If not, do you offer subsidies?

❑ Will you complete and submit all necessary paperwork to insurance companies?

Selecting an Assisted-Living Facility

Another long-term care alternative is assisted living. Assisted-living facilities may be part of a retirement community, a nursing home, elderly housing, or they may stand alone. Residents have their own living space; the companionship of others; programs, services, and often meals, along with various levels of assistance. You may also receive some medical services at home through assisted living. Whatever the setting, assisted living offers the opportunity to continue living as independently as possible.

Ask Yourself

❑ What part of town or what part of the country does this person want to live in?

❑ Is it important for her to be surrounded by her own furniture and other things that are familiar and memorable?

❑ Does she need access to public transportation?

❑ Does she want to buy or rent?

❏ Does she want to have social opportunities?

❏ What services does she want—meals, transportation, planned activities, housekeeping, laundry, nursing care?

Ask the Facility

❏ Is there a waiting list to get into this facility? How long?

❏ Are you a licensed facility?

❏ Are both furnished and unfurnished units available?

❏ What costs are included in the rate and which are extra? How much are the extra costs?

❏ Do you have subsidized units (if needed)?

❏ What kinds of services and programming are available? How easy or difficult is it to use the programming and services? Which services are provided on-site and which are contracted out?

❏ What kinds of activities and recreation are available? Do you provide transportation for shopping? Do you have field trips? Are there special-interest groups? Is there an extra cost for each event?

❏ Do you offer meals? Housekeeping?

❏ If meal allowances are included, can they be used at any time? If I don't use the entire meal allowance, can I bring guests in on my allowance?

❏ How often can guests come for meals?

❏ Can I get help for a short time if, say, I need a nurse for fifteen minutes? Can I choose the times?

❏ Are there common areas? Are there specific times they can be used?

❏ Are there certain hours for visitors?

❏ What kind of security does the building have?

❏ If the assisted-living building is part of a larger complex with long-term care, will I automatically be given a room for either short- or long-term care if I need it? Is there an extra fee? Do I have first choice of a bed?

❑ What happens if I need additional or more extensive assistance in a few years? Can this facility provide for such an event or will I have to find another facility?

❑ What happens if one person in a couple needs more extensive care? Do the living arrangements change?

❑ How friendly and welcoming are the residents in this building? Are there cliques that are hard to join?

❑ How do other residents treat a couple if one person has an illness?

Selecting a Nursing Home

The nursing home of yesterday has become a multipurpose facility; patients may be there for hospital recuperation, for respite care so their caretaker can have a break, for minimal services or more extensive services, or for long-term care.

Ask Yourself

❑ Do I understand the total health picture of the prospective resident?

❑ Is a nursing care facility the best place for him?

❑ What does he need and want in a facility?

❑ What is most important — service, the profile of the other residents, or proximity to family members?

❑ Do all family members and the potential resident agree about priorities?

❑ Am I honestly and clearly communicating the needs of the resident?

❑ Would he be happy with this facility if his level of required care changes?

Ask the Facility

❑ What is the profile of your residents? For example, are they mainly seniors, or are there younger people with physical and mental disabilities?

❑ How is the resident evaluated? What criteria determine the care level needed?

❑ What are the differences among levels of care?

❑ Do you have a patients' bill of rights?

❑ Does the admission contract include all the terms, even oral agreements?

❑ Do residents have input into their activities and policies through a resident council?

❑ Can residents go outside unattended? Are there outdoor sitting arrangements?

❑ Do you have an effective family council?

❑ How do you handle difficult residents? Do you use restraints?

Ask About Services

❑ What services do you offer: short-term care, respite care, long-term care for all levels of health needs?

❑ Are the services the resident needs coordinated to maximize her stay here?

❑ What therapies do you offer—physical, speech, occupational, art, pet therapy?

❑ Do you have special services or equipment for people who are vision or hearing impaired?

❑ What recreational activities do you offer?

❑ Do you offer outings? What determines who goes on an outing? How many staff and volunteers accompany the outings? Are you equipped to take people with special needs? Are there additional fees?

❑ How often are the residents bathed and groomed? Do they have an option of having a person of the same gender bathe them?

❑ How are residents kept informed of daily activities and of special events?

❑ Are there limitations on how many residents can attend activities and events? What criteria is used to determine who can attend?

❑ Can family members attend activities? Do they need to inform someone they will be attending?

❑ Do you have a beauty shop and canteen?

❑ Do you have floors for people who require intensive care? Do we pay more for this care?

❑ What religious services are available in this facility?

❑ What kind of support do you offer new families and residents?

❑ How often does your staff meet to discuss the needs of the resident? Who attends these meetings?

❑ How often will the family be updated about the progress of the resident?

❑ What are your volunteer needs and opportunities?

❑ Do you have a newsletter for residents or families?

Ask About Treatments

❑ If the resident is ill, do you call her personal physician? Do you have on-staff doctors?

❑ Do you have complete records of the resident's medication? May additional medication be administered without the doctor's consent?

❑ Who gives the patient medication?

❑ If medication needs to be administered at different times, will you do that?

❑ Is the staff informed about drug interactions? Will they know the procedures that accompany different medications such as taking them on an empty stomach or with food?

❑ Is the resident watched for adverse reactions to new medication?

❑ Is the family notified immediately if the resident is ill or needs to go to the hospital?

❑ If your staff thinks the resident needs treatment, do you first get her consent or the family's?

❑ If the resident becomes less well can she stay in the same room or might she be required to change rooms or floors?

Ask About Living Conditions

❑ Can the resident bring her own furniture?

❑ Are her personal belongings safe here? Do we register them when she moves in?

❑ How many private rooms are there? How easy are they to get?

❑ Can married people share a room?

❑ Is there privacy for a married couple if only one of them is a resident?

❑ Are there private areas if a resident wants to be alone?

❑ What criteria do you use to assign residents to a room, roommate, and floor? Can we have input into the selection?

❑ Will you be honest about a difficult roommate? Can we meet the person first? How many roommates has this person previously had? Have other roommates moved out? If so, why?

❑ What if a roommate is very noisy? Is that taken into consideration in room assignments?

❑ How easy is it to switch roommates?

❑ Do the residents have their own phones or share phones? What is the cost?

❑ Are a bed and room held for a resident if she goes to the hospital?

❑ Are there eating facilities on each floor or will the resident need to leave the floor to eat? How much time are they allowed for meals? Can they eat in their rooms? Do they get food choices? Do you provide one-on-one eating help if needed?

❑ How often is the resident's room cleaned?

Ask About Staff

❑ What is the ratio of staff to residents? What are the percentages of licensed nursing staff to aides? What percentage are full-time staff assigned to the same floor? What percentage are floaters?

❑ What is the staff turnover rate?

❑ Can we expect the resident to have the same staff working with her?

❑ Do all the staff receive job and human relations training?

❑ How does the staff handle disruptive people during meals?

❑ Is your staff trained in emergency procedures in case of fire, tornado, earthquake, or hurricane?

❑ What arrangements have you made to evacuate residents if there is an emergency?

❑ Who should the resident or family speak to if there is a problem?

❑ How do we best interact with the staff to get what we need?

Ask About Finances

❑ Are all services covered by medical assistance or insurance?

❑ Do you do all the paperwork regarding finances? Will any prepayments be necessary?

❑ Do residents have to surrender their assets to the facility?

❑ Do you require residents have an account to handle incidental expenses? How much money may a resident have in an account? How much money will she need monthly in addition to the facility cost? Who keeps track of the money? Are the families and resident notified about the balance in the account or if costs increase?

❑ When the resident dies, who gets any remaining money in the resident's account? Is everything done automatically?

❑ If the resident needs to be hospitalized, how are the costs handled?

DON'T FORGET

❑ Involve the person who is receiving care in decisions whenever possible.

❑ Get recommendations and support from people you know — physicians, hospital social workers, and staff at social service agencies.

❑ Ask for references.

❑ Use on-line forums like CompuServe to get advice and talk with people in similar situations.

❑ Call Eldercare Locator (1-800-677-1116) or the National Association of Area Agencies (202-296-8130) for referrals to agencies nearest you that deal with aging.

❑ Call the National Hospice Helpline (1-800-658-8898) for questions about hospice services.

❑ For information on nonprofit housing, contact the American Association of Homes and Services for the Aging, Communications Division, 901 E Street N.W., Suite 500, Washington, DC 20004-2037, 202-783-2242.

❑ Call your state agency on aging and talk to your local ombudsperson about a specific care facility you are considering. Ask if they have many complaints about the facility, the nature of the complaints, how complaints are resolved, and the conditions they find when they go visit.

❑ Check with your state's department of human services and department of health for general nursing home information.

❑ Talk with people you know who have encountered many different facilities—physicians, clergy, hospital social workers. If they have personal experience with the facility you are considering, ask what they like and don't like about it; if not, ask if they have heard any pros or cons about it from colleagues.

❑ Talk to other residents and their family members. What do they like about the facility, and what would they like to be different? What kind of problems have they had and how have they been resolved?

❑ If possible, talk with nurses and other staff. What do they like about their job and the facility? Do they think there is adequate staffing to give the patients proper care? How often does the administration interact with the staff? Do the top managers hear the day-to-day issues so their decisions are based on complete information?

❑ Visit the facility you are considering several times, at different times of the day and different days of the week. While you are there, observe carefully and thoughtfully. Watch how other residents are treated. Are people quick to tend to their needs? Are they treated pleasantly? How clean are the residents' rooms and the common areas? Notice the atmosphere in the eating area. Do residents seem happy? Are they groomed? Does the food look appealing?

❑ Attend a family council meeting if there is one.

❑ Once you select a residence, get everything in writing.

❑ Get to know the people who work with the resident; if you have problems ask them for help.

❑ Make sure your expectations are reasonable. You want the resident to have the very best but be realistic about what the environment can provide.

❑ Take concerns to the appropriate people.
❑ Remember that staff is usually overloaded; treat them respect-fully.

Planning a Funeral

My father died more than thirty years ago, soon after we had moved to Phoenix. Because we didn't know many people, we asked the hospital to recommend a funeral home. The fast-talking funeral director showed us what he called the Cadillac of caskets and then others that weren't as nice. We finally selected one that balanced our guilt and our budget. We were sending my father's body back to Minneapolis for burial. The casket we had chosen was so heavy we had to send the body back by train, which took several days. This delayed the funeral, which is against my religion's tradition (burial as quickly as possible). In Minneapolis we were told that we should have sent my father's body by plane in a bag (now they use shipping containers) and bought the casket on arrival. The man in Phoenix somehow neglected to suggest this option.

Lessons learned: Call your hometown funeral home first if you are out of town. It is easier to explore and understand all your options when you are not devastated by emotions and dealing with time constraints. Be careful whom you trust and give your power away to; not everyone is looking out for your best interest. When transporting a body, buy the casket at the destination.

Funerals are one of those facts of life we all need but seldom think much about. Ideally, you should learn about funeral arrangements before you have a need for them, especially if you want to compare prices. Prearrangements will assure your wishes are taken into account and also will make things much easier on the survivors.

Planning Your Own Funeral Arrangements

❑ Do I want to prepay for funeral arrangements by establishing a trust account or do I want to buy insurance to pay for the funeral arrangements? Does this include all costs, including cemetery plot, monument, and any cemetery fees?

❑ If I prepay and change my mind, can I get the money back?

❑ How is the interest that is earned on the money applied to the account? Do taxes have to be paid on the interest?

❑ Are the costs locked in if I prepay?

❑ Is the fund guaranteed if the funeral home goes out of business?

❑ Does what I am selecting meet religious requirements?

❑ Do I qualify for a government burial?

❑ If I buy insurance, how soon will my family receive the money to pay for the funeral?

❑ How much of the arrangements do I want to make: music, readings, obituary notice, flowers, donations to charities?

❑ Do I want to donate to a transplant organization?

❑ Have I told family members about my desires?

Planning Funeral Arrangements for Someone Else

❑ If the body is taken from a hospital or care facility, what happens to the deceased's personal belongings? If he was wearing any jewelry, who is responsible for taking the jewelry off and where will it be safely stored?

❑ Do we know his specific desires about funeral arrangements?

❑ Has he prepaid and preplanned his own funeral arrangements? Has he made provisions in his will for funeral costs?

❑ Should the body be cremated, buried, or entombed?

❑ Did he donate any body parts to a hospital or transplant organization? If yes, does the recipient agency cover or pay any amount toward funeral arrangements? How does that affect the arrangements we need to make and the date of the funeral?

❑ Does the deceased qualify for social security or veteran's burial benefits?

❑ Does his religious institution or fraternal organization have a burial society that may reduce costs?

❑ How much money can we afford and are we willing to spend?

❑ Do we understand the religious rules and traditions regarding burials? How might they affect our decisions? Do we want or need a specific funeral home because of religious or other reasons? What are the extra costs to comply with religious customs?

❑ Do we want services in a funeral home, religious establishment, or graveside?

❑ Do we want to compare prices from several places? (Funeral homes are legally obligated to provide prices over the phone.)

❑ What is included in the quoted price? What about cemetery and monument costs?

❑ Have we obtained detailed, prepurchase price information, including a general price list of all services available from the mortuaries we want to consider?

❑ Who should officiate at the service? Do we want friends, relatives, or clergy to eulogize the person? Do we want to invite people to speak at the funeral? Do we want to invite attendees to speak if they would like?

❑ Do we want music? What selections? Whom should we hire and how much do we want to spend on music?

❏ Whom do we want to carry the casket? Are there religious restrictions regarding who can be included?

❏ Do we want the body viewed? Just for immediate family or for everyone? Do we want the body displayed before the funeral and/or at the time of the funeral?

❏ Do we want to purchase flowers?

❏ How do we want friends and relatives to contribute: flowers, donations to specific charities or to the donor's choice, food, money for the family?

❏ Do we want a long obituary or a short notice? Should specific groups be alerted in the obituary such as unions or associations?

❏ Do we want to print a picture of the deceased?

❏ What is the best time for friends, family, and clergy to attend a funeral or memorial service?

❏ At the culmination of the funeral arrangements, have we received the statement of funeral goods and services selected?

Ask About Cremation

❏ Will the body be present at the service?

❏ If we want the body cremated after the funeral or memorial service can we rent a casket for the service?

❏ Do we want to keep the ashes?

❏ Do we need to purchase an urn? What are the options?

❏ Do we want to keep, bury, or scatter the ashes? Where? Do we need a permit to do this? What is the procedure and cost to obtain a permit?

When Selecting a Cemetery Plot or Entombment

❏ Where does the deceased want to be buried—near other family members, hometown?

❏ Do we want to place the casket in a mausoleum or bury it?

❏ Does my place of worship have its own cemetery or burial society?

❏ If I prepurchase a plot and decide I don't want it, what are the resale options?

❏ If I prepurchase a plot, will my family members have to incur other costs?

❏ What rules and regulations does the cemetery have?

❏ What are our options for upkeep? Can we pay yearly? What is the fee for perpetual care? What does the maintenance include?

❏ Are there any limitations as to the size of the marker? Are there rules about what can be planted or put at the grave?

❏ Does the marker need to be erected by or at a certain time?

❏ When is the marker placed? Do we have a special service when the marker is placed? What does that entail?

❏ How often is the cemetery open for visitors?

❏ How secure is the cemetery from vandalism?

❏ Is the cemetery responsible for any replacement costs if it is vandalized? Does my home owner's insurance cover cemetery vandalism?

DON'T FORGET

❏ Ideally, plan early and check out several places.

❏ Ask friends and relatives for funeral homes they have been satisfied with.

❏ Call your state funeral directors' association and local funeral home for pamphlets and information. Also, ask them about any reported complaints about a funeral home you are considering.

❏ Call your state department of health, mortuary science division, to check on credentials or file a complaint.

❏ Get information from the American Association of Retired Persons, 601 E Street N.W., Washington, DC 20049.

❏ Get consumer information from your attorney general's office.

❏ The Funeral Service Consumer Assistance Program is a service of the National Research and Information Center, an independent, nonprofit organization that researches and provides consumer information on death, grief, and funeral services. Contact FSCAP, National Research and Information Center, 2250 E. Devon Avenue, Suite 250, Des Plaines, IL 60018, 1-800-662-7666.

PART FIVE

Everyday Living

Purchasing
Products

When I bought blinds for my room, I was most concerned about the color and style. I never thought about what side the pulley would be on and, of course, it ended up on the wrong side. I never thought of asking about it. In fact, I never thought about the pulley at all. *Lessons learned*: Look at all aspects of a product. Ask what assumptions the seller might be making about the product and how you will use it. Ask if there are other decisions to be made that you should be making.

Technology is so advanced and changing so quickly it is difficult to make decisions. To make the decision-making process more complex, there is an abundance of brands and services to select from. You must identify needs, learn about what is available and currently under development, articulate your desires as clearly as possible and decide what is best for you. Find a good salesperson who will listen to your needs, explain and show you available options, and present you with the features and benefits of various choices.

In 1994 consumers spent more than $590 billion on durable goods. You need to decide how much time and energy you want to expend researching each product you buy.

Some purchases may not be as important to you as others. When I bought my dishwasher I didn't even look at options. A friend sold dishwashers at a department store, so I asked her some questions and had one sent out. But when I purchased my computer I went in and out of stores, spoke to many people, and tried to make the best decision. In either case, make sure that you purchase from a reputable dealer who will assist you if you have any problems.

Ask Yourself

❑ Why do I need this product?

❑ What do I need it to do? What function will it serve?

❑ Do I want or need the most technically advanced, or top-of-the-line product?

❑ Which features are important to me—functions, materials it's made of, ease of use, ease of cleaning, ease of assembly and installation, noise level?

❑ Have I carefully measured the depth, width, and length of my space? Have I considered door openings and the amount of space I need to move this product into my residence? To comfortably use the product?

❑ Is this one of those products where extra costs such as installation could make a big difference in the price? If so can I find a more expensive product with less expensive extra costs? Do I need to make sure I get the total price as I explore options?

❑ Do I need help in making this decision? Do I want to hire an adviser to help me make this decision?

❑ How much time do I want to spend researching this product?

❑ How many product options do I want to explore?

❑ How many businesses that sell the product do I want to check for prices? Will the price, payment terms, warranty, or service influence where I buy?

❏ Would I be interested in a used product?

❏ Will I need additional circuits for this product?

❏ If the product is a replacement, are there differences that might influence my purchase (is it bigger, thicker, or wider)?

❏ Can I buy this product cheaper through my credit union, club, or business?

❏ What financing options are available to me—credit union, home improvement loan, other type of loan, store financing?

❏ Have I read the contract clearly? Are all the terms we agreed upon written in the contract?

Ask the Vendor

❏ How long have you been in business?

❏ Is there a wide range of models? What are the benefits of each model?

❏ Are any of these going to be discontinued? Will parts still be available if this model is discontinued?

❏ Comparing your product to the competition, in terms of product, service, and price, what do you have that they don't? What do they have that you don't?

❏ What are the advantages and disadvantages of upgrading? Will this product be able to utilize new technology?

❏ If I am unhappy with any of my selections [if purchasing through a new home builder or wholesaler] can I change without paying a restock charge?

❏ What colors are available? Does the model I want come in the color I want?

❏ Do I have choices about the location of different parts—the pulley on the window treatment, the control panel in a car, which way the door opens?

❏ Are there any hidden costs that can make a difference?

❏ Are there choices of materials that different parts are made of? What are the advantages and liabilities of the different materials? How easily will they scratch or chip?

❏ Does this product have any electrical requirements that I need to know about? Does it need to be a certain distance from other electrical appliances to avoid interference?

❏ Does it need ventilation room?

❏ Does it require a certain kind of lighting to avoid glare?

❏ What is standard and what is optional? Are there extras that I can purchase later? Will the extras fit internally or will I need to use them externally (such as a CD ROM)? What are the advantages of having the extras internal or external?

❏ Will this product fit comfortably into the space I've planned?

❏ What is the ease of using this product? Does it fit my needs, such as wide shelves in the freezer to hold frozen pizza?

❏ What is the average life of this product?

❏ Are there other features that aren't shown that may be special ordered? Do I pay more for special ordering?

❏ Do you have this product in stock? If not, how long will it take for me to get? Will I pay more for a special order?

❏ Is there a trial period or rental option so I can try this first?

❏ What kind of complaints and feedback have you had about this product? Has this product been recalled?

❏ What is your return policy? Is there a money-back guarantee?

❏ What can I do if I am not satisfied? Do your contracts specify conflict resolution methods such as arbitration?

❏ How reliable is this product? What percentage of buyers have problems with it in the first year?

❏ What parts may wear out quickly? What is the replacement cost?

❏ Will there be any unusual odors from this product? If yes, how long will the smell last?

❑ If a used product, how are you sure the product hasn't received more use than you were told? Can I contact the previous owners? What have you done to fix the product? Can I take it and have it assessed by a professional or bring a professional in to look at it?

❑ Are there people available if I need help in using the product? How accessible are they? How quickly will they return calls and find solutions?

❑ What company manufactures the goods? Is the company involved in activities that I approve of or not (is it a union company, does it contaminate other countries, exploit workers, support community activities)?

❑ Who serves on the board of directors? Does the board reflect my values?

Ask About Delivery

❑ What are the delivery charges? Are they per item or for the total purchase?

❑ Does the charge include installation?

❑ Do you remove the old appliance or product? Are there additional fees for removal?

❑ When will you deliver the product?

❑ Might there be a clearance problem in bringing this into my home?

❑ Do I have to pay more for having it taken up or down steps?

Ask About Assembly or Installation

❑ How easy is this to put together or install?

❑ Does it require special tools or supplies?

❑ Do you have staff to assemble it? What would be the additional cost?

❑ Are all the necessary parts included?

❑ Will there be installation problems if changes have been made since the first product was installed? For example, if a new kitchen floor has been installed there might be a problem removing the dishwasher.

Ask About Warranties

❑ Does obtaining a warranty make good financial sense?

❑ What does the warranty include? Does it cover more than defects? Does it cover service calls?

❑ Are extended warranties available? What do they include? Do they cover the cost of service calls?

❑ Does my credit card company or bank give warranties and purchase insurance if I use their card or checks when I make a purchase?

❑ Can I get service contracts from other places, such as the gas company, that may be better and less expensive?

❑ What are the chances of this product needing repairs during the warranty time?

❑ Where is service done? How long does service usually take? Are parts readily obtainable? How easy is the product to service if I'm traveling with it? If I move to another part of the country? To a different country?

Ask About Finances

❑ Is this item going to be on sale in the near future? Can I get the sale price now? Will you be offering any special payment options in the near future?

❑ Do you match prices if I can find this cheaper somewhere else?

❑ Do special financial promotions apply to all priced products?

❑ What is the total cost of my purchase, including installation, delivery, taxes, any other extras?

❑ Do you offer a lease option? What is the total cost if I lease? What is the cost if I pay cash? Finance it?

❑ Are there any manufacturer rebates?

❑ Are there any catches to no-interest payments or extended payment plans? If I don't pay off the total amount in the allotted time period, will the entire interest be retroactive?

❑ If low financing is available, am I paying more for the product to get the financing? Is the down payment higher to get this financing? Do I have to buy additional products to get the financing? What are the purchase and delivery time limits on this financial offer?

Ask About Leasing a Product

❑ Are there financial advantages to leasing?

❑ Will the money I spend on rental apply to the purchase price?

❑ What are the terms? How many payments? What happens if I am late with a payment?

❑ Will I be getting a new or used product?

❑ Does the price include installation and delivery?

❑ Is there a penalty or extra charges if I pay the lease off early?

❑ Are there any fees due at the end of the contract?

❑ Are there any use limits in the lease? What happens if I exceed those limits? What is the normal wear and tear expected? What if my use of the product exceeds the normal wear standards?

❑ What will I pay if I want to buy the product at the end of the lease? If the market value is less at the end, will the price be adjusted?

❑ What happens if the product is damaged or stolen during the leasing period? Do I need special insurance?

Ask About Mail Order

❑ Do you have the item in stock currently? If not, how long until I can expect to have this item delivered?

❏ Is this item going on sale anytime soon? What if I purchase it and I see it discounted in your next catalog?

❏ What is your return policy?

❏ What form of payment do you accept?

❏ What happens if I'm not satisfied with this item? Do you offer refunds or credits only?

❏ What are the applicable taxes?

❏ Who does your shipping?

❏ What are the shipping costs? Will I save on shipping if I buy multiple items or have a higher total cost?

❏ How long does shipping take? Will I be notified of any shipping delays?

❏ Can I have the item shipped to another address?

❏ What happens if the item is damaged during shipping? What do I have to do to get a replacement?

❏ Are there any other charges?

❏ What if I find this same item elsewhere for a lower price? Will you match it? What kind of proof do you need?

❏ Will I be added to your mailing list?

❏ Will you sell my name to other companies? Do I have the option to stay off such lists?

DON'T FORGET

❏ Take time to consider any purchase. Think about all aspects of the product.

❏ Check financing before you purchase; your bank might have a better payment plan than a dealer.

❏ Get the purchase price on a product before you ask about leasing.

❏ Scrutinize payment plans; you could be paying a lot more for a leasing arrangement.

❑ Call the manufacturer and ask what kind of complaints they have had about their product.

❑ Inspect the specific item carefully. If it looks like it has been returned, ask why.

❑ Use the consumer forum on CompuServe or other information networks for general advice; ask if a specific product has been problematic.

❑ Research by reading *Consumer Reports*, *Consumer's Digest*, and other consumer publications.

❑ Check the Better Business Bureau regarding the company.

❑ Call the attorney general's office for any information published about the product you want to buy. Ask if there is any litigation against the company you want to buy from.

❑ Understand laws that may govern your purchase. For example, the U.S. Postal Service and the Federal Trade Commission govern mail-order purchases. There may be state "Lemon Laws" that protect you. The Federal Trade Commission also has rules and guidelines for the purchase of other types of products and services. Call your local office and ask for a copy of the booklet *Facts for Consumers*.

❑ If you are told insurance or Medicare will cover your purchase, check with the carrier first.

❑ Charge your purchase; don't pay for it if you are unhappy.

❑ Be careful of size designation like large or extra large on appliances. Get clear information about what that means in terms of capacity.

❑ Buy a surge protector for a computer.

❑ When buying from a mail-order company, keep a copy of your order form.

Hiring a
Repair Person

I bought a desk that my handyman said he could assemble. It took him several hours to construct it since he had never done anything like it before. Later, I discovered I could have hired experienced people at a lower rate. I thought I was saving money, but it ended up costing me more. *Lessons learned*: Ask what experience the person has had in doing the exact or similar work. Ask how much it will cost to have something assembled in-house. There are some people who like challenges and will lead you to believe something is easy when it may not be. Ask approximately how long it will take to assemble the item. Ask if the person charges for the time it takes to figure something out and to fix mistakes. What may seem to be an easier way is often not the best way.

Ideally one hires service or repair people who have been recommended by satisfied customers you trust. Sometimes it is hard to find reliable people and you may be so anxious to get the work done that you settle for what you can get.

Be certain that the person you hire will actually be doing the work. Once I hired a painter who was recommended, but he sent inexperienced college students to do a job instead.

Ask Yourself

❑ Am I sure I want to do this?

❑ What are my expectations for a completed job?

❑ Have I clearly communicated my expectations?

❑ Does the person I am hiring understand my expectations? Has he acknowledged that the expectations are realistic and achievable?

❑ Does the contract contain all my wants and expectations?

❑ Why is this person less costly or more costly than other bidders?

Ask the Repair Person

❑ How long have you been in business?

❑ Will you be working on this project yourself?

❑ What are your qualifications?

❑ If others are working on the project, what are their qualifications?

❑ Have you done this type of work before?

❑ Are you registered, bonded, insured?

❑ Is there a money-back guarantee?

❑ Do you charge a flat rate or hourly rate?

❑ What type of payment arrangements do you have?

❑ Why is your bid lower than others? How are you cutting costs?

❑ What kind of guarantee is there?

❑ What recourse do I have if I am not satisfied?

❑ Are there extra costs?

❑ Do you carry liability insurance?

❑ Do we need any special permits from the city? Will you get them? What do they cost? Am I responsible for any of this cost?

❑ Have you used this product before?

❑ Who will oversee the project? Make sure the workers are prompt? Doing a good job? Keep me current on the progress?

❑ When will you start the project? When will you finish? What circumstances might affect the completion date?

❑ Will you sign a contract giving a written completion date?

❑ Will you initial the contract when details are rewritten?

❑ Can I add a holdback clause and give you the final payment after I have had the job inspected?

❑ Can you cite me an example of a problem or misunderstanding you had with a customer and how you handled it?

❑ What is the life of the product or repair?

❑ What are other product or repair options?

❑ Why have you selected this product?

❑ Do you clean up after yourself, removing all leftover materials and any dirt you may have created?

❑ Do you have references I may contact?

DON'T FORGET

❑ Call references.

❑ Call the Better Business Bureau.

❑ Get everything in writing.

❑ Make sure the performance matches your agreement.

❑ Check to see that any products used are consistent with your agreement.

❑ Don't pay the final bill until you are sure the work is according to your agreement and acceptable.

Selecting a Long-Distance Telephone Service

When my publisher asked me to include questions to ask a long-distance provider, I had no idea how much information I was going to find and that it would save me money. I called my provider with questions and said I was thinking of switching companies. The customer service representative asked me to hold the line. When she returned, she said, "You have been with us a long time and we don't want to lose your business. Would it be okay if we gave you free long-distance phone calls the first weekend of each month (up to three hundred dollars worth) for six months and the seventh month would be totally free?" It was an enticing offer, so I agreed. But my main concern was making long-distance phone calls from a location other than my home. This company's surcharge was quite high. So I asked the representative if I could get anything less expensive and if they offered prepaid cards. She said they did not. But I had read in an article that this company recently introduced them. I called back and spoke to a different person. She told me that my phone company did offer prepaid cards. However, she didn't have the details of this offer so she referred me to a number where I could get this information. I decided to stay with my long-distance phone company since I was able to get a prepaid card and avoid the surcharge and receive free long-distance calls as a bonus.

I was happy for a while until I priced a call from my home to Mexico where my daughter was taking classes. My provider charged three times more than a competing company. When I called to complain, I was told about a special deal where I could pay a nominal monthly fee that would greatly reduce the charges for my international calls. *Lessons learned*: There are many options for long-distance service even in the same company. Know your own phone needs and patterns. If you are considering changing phone service, tell your current company. They may offer you a bonus to keep you as a customer. Explore all your choices asking specific questions. Call the same company twice and ask the same questions of another representative. Companies don't always keep their employees well informed and changes occur rapidly. Don't be attracted to a rate or service that doesn't meet your needs. As your needs change, reassess your program and provider. Know that there are reseller long-distance companies that may be able to offer you lower rates attuned to your long-distance usage habits.

Be aware of scams (called slamming in this industry) aimed at getting you to switch carriers. If a company asks if they can send you information, make sure they understand you are not making a switch, just agreeing to review their information.

Ask Yourself

❑ What are my calling needs and patterns? Do I make a lot of long-distance calls? At certain times? Days? To specific individuals? Locations? Do I make many international calls? In-state calls? Out-of-state calls?

❑ Is there a better carrier to use? Are there other, good options to the big three?

❑ What are my bills now? Do I want them evaluated by different companies?

Ask Providers About Plans

❑ In addition to your basic plan, what discount plans do you offer? Are there discounts based on the amount of the total bill? Calling specific numbers? Time call is placed? Distance? Any other criteria?

❑ Do you have minimum use requirements or is a surcharge levied?

❑ How much are calls during the day? Evening? Weekend?

❑ Is there a special deal if I frequently call the same area code but not the same number?

❑ Do you offer a discounted international calling package? Is there a fee? How much?

❑ Can I get additional discounts for the most commonly called number?

❑ Can discounts fluctuate monthly? What determines the discounted rate?

❑ Do you have a flat rate that applies all the time? Do I have to pay a monthly fee for that service?

❑ Are there different rates for in-state and out-of-state calls?

❑ Do you charge by the minute or smaller increments? How does that affect my charges?

❑ Do you offer free long-distance calls on certain days of the year, such as holidays or days I specify? Are these calls limited to people who subscribe to your service?

❑ Do I need special access numbers? Will I need to use an access code from home?

❑ Do I need special access numbers if I make calls overseas to the U.S. or other countries?

❑ Do you provide an 800 collect-call number? What are the costs for the number? What are the benefits?

❑ Do I have to pay a fee to my local telephone company if I switch long-distance carriers? Do you reimburse me for the fee? If I am unhappy with your service will you pay to switch me back?

❑ Will you look at my last few bills and compare your prices to what I paid?

❑ Do I get anything for signing up as a new customer?

❑ Are there bonus rewards like airline miles on your monthly bills?

❑ If considering a reseller, do you buy from more than one company? What are my choices?

❑ Can I get a copy of our agreement in writing?

❑ I am thinking of switching companies; is there anything you want to offer me to retain my business?

❑ Do you provide a calling card? Is there a surcharge for using it? Are there larger surcharges if I make international calls from other countries?

❑ Is the fee per minute more, less, or the same using a calling card? Is the fee for using the calling card a flat rate or determined by other factors?

❑ Do you have prepaid calling cards? In what denominations can I buy them? What is the per-minute charge of a call using this card? Where can I buy them? Can I use them anywhere? Do you have prepaid international calling cards? Does the card inform me when I will be running out of time? Is it the cheapest option if I am calling long distance away from home?

❑ To avoid anyone else using my card, do you have a service that allows me to make calls based on my voice and predetermined information? What is the extra cost for that service?

❑ Do you offer informational lines to call for the weather, soap opera updates, horoscopes, or other topics of interest? What is the cost per minute?

❑ Do you have a service where I can leave a message with your company to call a party at a certain time and deliver my message which will be in my voice? Will you keep calling the party to ensure they receive the message? How often? What is the cost for this service?

❏ Do you have multilingual operators?

DON'T FORGET

❏ Talk to friends and family to find out which long-distance telephone service they use and why.

❏ Ask each company you are considering to compare their rates to the charges on your current long-distance bill.

❏ For a list of resellers in your area, write to the Telecommunications Resellers Association, 1155 Connecticut Avenue N.W., Washington, DC 20036.

❏ For easy comparison shopping send $2 and a self-addressed stamped envelope to TRAC, P.O. Box 12038, Washington, DC 20005 for a copy of "Tele-Tips."

❏ If you have been slammed (victimized by a long-distance calling scam), write to the Federal Communication Commission, Enforcement Division, Common Carrier Bureau, 2025 M Street N.W., Washington, DC 20554.

Selecting a Doctor

Several years ago my mother became ill. She hired a doctor who had successfully treated me. She was so happy this doctor cured me that she put complete faith in him. After examining her, the doctor recommended surgery without explaining to her that her illness was cancer-related. After the surgery he came out and announced my mother's cancer had spread and she had only three months to live. Words can't express how I felt. I had no idea my mother had cancer. A close doctor friend of mine who looked at my mother's chart said that the other doctor knew my mother had cancer before her surgery. Yet no one told us. When we hired an oncologist he said that if he had been brought in for the surgery, he would have performed a procedure that could have given my mother more time. I asked, doesn't our doctor know about these things. He said yes and that he had told him several times about this alternative procedure but he said the other doctor doesn't seem to pay attention. He said oncologists see patients for a longer time and can evaluate the effect of treatments, whereas surgeons don't continue with the patient. *Lessons learned:* Because a doctor (or anyone for that matter) is competent in one area doesn't mean he is competent in another. Ask very specific questions and if you think someone is not giving you all the information you have a right to know, call him on it. Get more than one opinion. Learn about the latest research. Hire a doctor who you can relate to, one who is open and communicative.

Ask Yourself

❑ What qualities do I want in a doctor — good bedside manner, credentials, compassion, good communication skills, patience?

❑ Do I want a specialist or generalist?

❑ Do I care about the gender of the doctor? Age? Other criteria?

❑ Do I want a doctor in a small practice or large clinic?

❑ Are location and access to transportation important?

❑ Do I want a clinic that is open evenings, weekends?

❑ Do I want the doctor I go to to use a certain hospital?

❑ Do I want to have a choice in the doctors I see?

❑ What are my insurance guidelines? Requirements? Limitations? Is the doctor that I want a member of my HMO? If not, can I still be treated by him? What additional costs will this entail?

❑ Who do I want to be told about my illness?

❑ Who do I want the doctor to discuss my case with?

❑ Do I want a living will? Have I given copies of it to my health care provider, nearest relative, and hospital?

Ask the Doctor or Medical Office

❑ What are your credentials? Specialties? Are you board certified? What are your professional affiliations?

❑ Will you work as a team with my other physicians? Are you on staff at the same hospitals?

❑ How does your office handle emergencies? How easy is it to see you in case of illness or emergency? Who are the doctors that cover emergencies? Are they your associates? What are their credentials?

❏ How much time is needed to make an appointment for a routine checkup?

❏ How quickly are calls returned?

❏ How much time will you spend with me during an appointment? Do you leave enough time open for acute illnesses?

❏ What kind of facilities and equipment do you have to perform lab work and procedures in the office? Is your lab accredited?

❏ What insurance do you accept?

❏ Do I have to pay a co-payment at the time of a visit or am I billed?

❏ Do I have to pay for a missed appointment? What is your cancellation policy?

❏ Do you accept Medicare assignments?

❏ Do you have plans to relocate or retire soon?

❏ If you need to refer me to specialists, can I select my own? Are there certain specialists I must see?

❏ What is your treatment orientation? Would you consider yourself conservative or aggressive? Are you proactive with preventive measures? How do you feel about alternative forms of medicine such as acupuncture, homeopathic, or chiropractic care?

❏ Do you treat symptoms or look at the total picture?

❏ Do you take the time to explain the cause of the illness or condition to your patients?

❏ How do you keep current on the latest research? Where can I find out about research I may be interested in?

❏ What hospitals are you affiliated with?

❏ How important is patient satisfaction to you?

❏ Are your staff trained on the job or certified in their fields?

Ask About Treatments

❑ What are my options?

❑ For each treatment option, what is its success rate? Potential side-effects? Risks? Benefits?

❑ Where can I go for second or even third opinions?

❑ How will I know if a treatment is helping me? How soon will I see a difference?

❑ Do I need a specialist? If not, how often do you handle these types of cases?

❑ Are there periodic evaluations of the treatment?

❑ What is my prognosis?

Ask About Hospitalization

❑ What are the benefits and liabilities of different types of anesthesia?

❑ Is the total cost of my room covered by hospitalization insurance?

❑ What costs aren't covered by insurance?

❑ How much extra is a private room?

❑ Will I need cash on hand for things like the daily newspaper? Any other fees?

❑ Are there patient advocates working in the hospital? How do I contact them?

❑ Is smoking allowed in the hospital? Can I request a nonsmoking or smoking room?

❑ What are the visiting hours? Can family members come earlier and stay later?

❑ What kind of care and attention will I receive after surgery? Will the nurses look in on me more often after surgery?

❑ If I want a private nurse or aide around the clock, how do I go about hiring one? What will it cost?

❏ Will I need a special diet? For how long?

❏ Can the kitchen meet dietary preferences? Can I order food other than the choices I am offered?

❏ Is there a place at the hospital or nearby for family members to stay?

❏ May a family member sleep in my room?

❏ Will the hospital permit cultural or religious ceremonies that I would like performed?

DON'T FORGET

❏ At your first meeting, notice the doctor's attitude and behavior. Does he seem willing to take time to talk with you, or does he seem rushed? Is he condescending to you? Your family? Does he mind you asking questions? Does he support getting additional opinions? Does he ask about your family history? Does he ask about medications you are taking?

❏ Notice the actions of the office staff. Are they polite, friendly, and accommodating?

❏ Know your doctor's success rate for a given procedure, and talk with others if you are unsure.

❏ Use the hospital's library, if there is one.

❏ Contact the American Board of Medical Specialties (1-800-776-2378) to verify credentials of specialists.

❏ If applicable, call the American Cancer Society (1-800-227-2345) for information about cancer prevention, detection, and treatment options, available resources, or other assistance.

❏ Call the Block Cancer Hotline (1-816-932-8453) to receive support from other cancer patients, information referral, or free publications.

❏ Call the National Cancer Institute (1-800-422-6237) for information on the latest cancer research, state-of-the-art treatment options, explanations of technical medical terms, or for help formulating questions to ask your doctors.

❑ If applicable, contact the National Institute on Aging, Information Center, P.O. Box 8057, Gaithersburg, MD 20898–8057 for helpful brochures or referrals.

❑ If applicable, contact the Arthritis Foundation, P.O. Box 19000, Atlanta, GA 30326, and ask for their free brochure "Unproven Remedies."

❑ If applicable, contact the Alzheimer's Association, 919 N. Michigan Avenue, Suite 1000, Chicago, IL 60611, 1–800-272–3900.

Hiring an Attorney

When my daughter was injured in a tornado at camp, I hired a personal injury attorney. I thought I took all the right steps to find a good attorney—I observed him in court, I asked other attorneys about him, and I interviewed him. As my daughter improved and the case was worth less money, he turned the case over to another attorney—someone I would never hire. I was appalled. His response to me was, "When you hired me you hired my entire law firm." Had I known this, I would not have selected this firm.

I expect to choose who works for me and be comfortable with that person and his abilities. Since the appeal of the case diminished as my daughter healed, I couldn't find another attorney to take it. I became a victim in this situation. I had the option to work with an attorney I didn't choose or have no attorney at all. *Lessons learned*: Make sure the person you hire is going to be working the case. Meet others who may be working on the case. Talk to a few attorneys before you hire one and ask how they will be developing the case.

When people need to hire an attorney they are often unhappy about a situation, perhaps feeling victimized, vulnerable, and angry. They want someone to help. Since there is more than one way to interpret the law and people have different styles, you want to maximize your chances of hiring an attorney who is not only competent but who feels comfortable to you.

Ask Yourself

❑ Do I really need an attorney? Have I communicated clearly with the other party and tried to negotiate a mutually acceptable solution without involving lawyers?

❑ Is there a small claims court I can go to instead?

❑ Is there some type of arbitration or mediation I can try first?

Ask the Attorney

❑ What are your credentials?

❑ How long have you practiced law?

❑ Do you have a specialty?

❑ Do you know the opposing attorney (if a case has been filed)? If so, what kind of working relationship do you have with this attorney?

❑ Is your negotiation style collaborative or competitive?

❑ What percentage of your cases go to court? What percentage are settled out of court?

❑ What percentage of your cases do you remove yourself from before completion?

❑ What percentage of your clients dismiss you before a case is resolved?

❑ Do you do most of the work on your cases? Will others (paralegals, law clerks, other attorneys) be involved in the case? If so, what are their qualifications and roles?

❑ Who will I mainly be working with? If this case goes to court, will you be representing me?

❑ Do you charge for an initial interview?

❑ What is your hourly rate?

❏ If the fee is based on winning the case (contingency fee), are there other expenses that will come out of the settlement?

❏ What other fees and costs are there? Will I be charged for copies, postage, long-distance phone calls, and other case-related items?

❏ Do I pay for other personnel involved in the case? What are their hourly rates?

❏ Do you charge for the time we talk on the phone? At what rate?

❏ What type of payment arrangements are there?

❏ When is the money due?

❏ Do you send me an itemized monthly statement of costs?

❏ If we win the case and you ask the court to have the opposing (losing) side pay my attorney's fees, is this the final amount you will be asking for or will there be other costs?

❏ Have you managed similar cases?

❏ What is the worst scenario for my case? What is the best scenario?

❏ What are the chances of the worst scenario happening? What are the chances of the best scenario happening?

❏ What is your track record with the judge who has been assigned to this case?

❏ What kind of reputation does the assigned judge have in handling my type of case?

❏ Can I ask to have a different judge assigned? Might I get a worse judge?

❏ What do you think my chances are of winning this case?

❏ What are the relevant dates and deadlines for the case?

❏ What is your client service philosophy? How involved do you like and expect your clients to be?

❏ Are phone calls returned promptly?

❏ How am I kept current on my case?

❑ How am I involved in planning the strategy for presenting my case?

❑ Who will be the main person responsible for the case? Who will be my contact when I want information?

❑ If I am deposed, what is the process?

❑ If the attorney representing the opposing side asks an inappropriate question, will you object? Can I?

❑ What is my recourse if the opposing attorney is intimidating, shaming, or abusive to me?

DON'T FORGET

❑ Look around for people who have been satisfied with their attorneys and ask them why.

❑ Check out attorneys you are considering by calling the professional ethics committee of your county bar association. Ask other attorneys and court personnel about their experiences with this law firm and attorney. Judges are human; if you choose an attorney with a bad reputation you could bias your own case. Be careful of attorneys that laypeople consider good just because they charge a high rate.

❑ Interview several attorneys. Try to select one who can feel compassion toward you because he has experienced something similar or knows people who have but doesn't have an ax to grind.

❑ Beware of attorneys who make you promises about outcomes they might not be able to produce. Remember that judges and juries determine the outcome of cases. The attorney's job is to maximize your chances of obtaining a settlement in your favor.

❑ Gain an understanding of the process.

❑ Make sure you are involved with and understand all the decisions that affect your case.

❑ Ask for all sides of an issue—strengths, weaknesses, pros, and cons.

❑ Get a clear, concise contract with your attorney.

❑ Listen carefully to the attorney's tone and for other signs that indicate personality or style traits—angry, forceful, or competitive—that you might not be comfortable with.

❑ Watch to assure that your attorney is behaving and producing in the ways promised. If not, confront her or fire her and find someone else.

❑ Watch to see that your attorney is willing to negotiate. The attorney's fee may be larger if the case goes to court. Try to settle quickly in an amicable manner.

❑ Keep current on the case. Ask if you don't hear.

❑ Ask for schedules.

❑ Watch deadlines.

Selecting Alternative Dispute Resolutions

After my daughter was injured at camp, I was involved in a personal injury lawsuit. My attorney asked us to go to non-binding arbitration. He said it might be a way to get a settlement without going to court; if we didn't like the outcome we could go to court. I agreed to this. When the day arrived, my attorney presented an extremely weak case and seemed quite unprepared. This arbitration did not come out in my favor. Soon thereafter my attorney dropped the case. It didn't occur to me that non-binding arbitration was a way for him to gauge whether the law firm wanted to spend money on my case or whether he would drop my case. Had I known these things, I probably would not have agreed to arbitration. In retrospect, I think that mediation — where the involved parties participate in the decision-making process — would have been more appropriate for me than a lawsuit. I was more concerned that the camp change their procedures than with a financial settlement. My attorneys, who worked on a contingency-fee basis, were more concerned about money.

Alternative dispute resolution, which focuses on the needs and interests of the concerned parties, is becoming the preferred option for many legal conflicts. Litigation, the traditional form of dispute resolution, is often costly, adversarial — because there is usually a winner and loser—and time consuming. Alternative dispute resolution may help the parties involved reach a mutually agreeable outcome. Here's an example of how alternative dispute resolution could help address the needs and interests of both parties involved in a way that traditional litigation cannot. Two sisters both want the last orange in the refrigerator. After arguing, they compromised by splitting it in half. As it turned out, one sister wanted to make juice from the orange and the other sister wanted to use the peel for a cake recipe. The way they shared the orange, neither sister had enough to complete her task. If the sisters had discussed their needs and interests beforehand, they might have. Conflict does not necessarily have a right and wrong answer but can be based on different expectations, needs, and values. It makes sense to explore options that can benefit both parties.

However, alternative dispute resolution is not appropriate in all cases. Nor are the people performing it necessarily good at it. Also, because this process is in its infancy, each state has different procedural guidelines.

Lessons learned: Define what you want out of a case and learn the options available to achieve your outcome. Understand and know the full ramifications of any alternative dispute resolution process that you use. Know the qualifications of the person conducting the alternative dispute resolution procedure and whether the person has had experience with your kind of case before. Use an attorney or representative that you feel is trustworthy.

To Select a Conflict Resolution Option, Ask Yourself

❑ Have we reached a point where others need to be involved?

❑ Do I know anyone who could help settle this dispute?

❑ Would I prefer to have this dispute settled out of court?

❑ What is my desired outcome from this case? Is this realistic?

❑ Do I have some underlying issues I am not recognizing or admitting? Do I really want a resolution?

❏ Am I willing to discuss all the issues of this dispute?

❏ Do I want to use this case to establish precedent? If so, is court my only option?

❏ What are my own limitations in dealing with this conflict? Am I willing to work toward a win-win outcome?

❏ Do I want to consider alternative dispute resolution?

❏ Do I want arbitration, where the outcome is decided by a third party?

❏ Do I want mediation, where I can participate in the decision-making process?

❏ Do I want to consider other options such as mini-trials, negotiation, ombudsperson, or a combination of mediation and arbitration?

❏ Does my state require me to go through mediation or arbitration before a court hearing? Do I need to file a claim such as a human rights violation?

❏ Are there organizations in my community that may help me resolve this problem, such as a human rights commission?

❏ Does my community offer free mediation services? Will anyone assess whether this case is appropriate for alternative dispute resolution?

❏ Does my community organization use volunteers? Are the volunteers experienced with the kind of issues I am dealing with?

❏ Do I or does the other party belong to an association that offers a dispute resolution process we can use?

❏ Is there a time limit effecting the use of mediation or arbitration?

❏ Am I comfortable entering the mediation or arbitration process without an attorney or adviser or should I have an attorney represent me in this process?

❏ What is my best alternative to a negotiated agreement? What is my worst alternative to a negotiated agreement?

❑ Am I open to hearing how the other person perceives the dispute and his needs?

❑ Will I be comfortable in a face-to-face meeting?

❑ Am I free to settle this dispute or will I need the input of others who might not be present?

❑ How important is confidentiality to me?

❑ What qualities are important for me to have in a mediator? Are there gender concerns I might have in this selection? Would two mediators or a panel be better in this situation?

❑ What are my expectations of mediation? Do I expect the mediation to deal with emotional issues?

❑ Can I have input into the selection of a mediator?

❑ Do I need or want an attorney as a mediator or would I prefer a lay person or a person with expertise in the field?

❑ Can the mediation take place during hours that are convenient for me?

❑ Are there any fees involved for mediation? Arbitration?

❑ Are there cultural differences between the disputants that may affect our choice of resolution and who is present?

❑ If I don't agree to go through the dispute resolution, will it affect how the court views my case?

❑ As a victim, what would I like the other party to agree to: some type of restitution, incarceration, community service, or other options?

Ask About Alternative Dispute Resolution

❑ How and where can I have this dispute evaluated to determine if it is a good case for alternative dispute resolution?

❑ How long would I have to wait to resolve this conflict through alternative dispute resolution? Court?

❑ Where will the dispute resolution take place? Can I have input into the selection of a location?

❑ Will it cost me less or more money to use this process than going to court?

❑ Does this process have to be done face-to-face or can the parties meet separately with the appropriate people?

❑ How will payments be handled?

❑ Is there a filing fee in addition to an hourly fee?

❑ How are costs handled if the process takes longer than anticipated?

❑ What procedures and process do you view as standard? Can I have input into determining the procedures and process we use to resolve this case?

❑ How will you recognize if there is not equal bargaining power? What would you do to attempt to equalize it?

❑ Can the process be private and confidential?

Ask About Arbitration

❑ What determines whether I need to go to arbitration before a court hearing—dollar amount, prearranged agreement, legalities?

❑ Is this a nonbinding arbitration where I can appeal the decision?

❑ Can the other party also appeal the decision? Is this a case where the other party is bound to the decision but I can appeal?

❑ Do I have any input into selecting the arbitrator?

❑ Is there a benefit to using a panel rather than one arbitrator?

❑ What are the procedures?

❑ Would it be helpful to have subject matter experts as part of the process?

❑ Can the parties bring expert witnesses into the arbitration?

❑ Is there a fee for arbitration?

❑ If I or the other party decide to go to court after the arbitration, will the party deciding to litigate have to incur extra costs if the court does not produce a more favorable result?

❑ What will influence the arbitrator's decision? How important is the law or evidence to the arbitrator in making a decision?

❑ How long will the arbitration last?

❑ When will I hear the decision about this case?

Ask About Mediation and the Mediator

❑ If seeking mediation services through an organization, do you have mediators that are experienced in my type of case? Do you help me assess my needs and explain my options?

❑ What role will you play—facilitator, problem solver, negotiator, evaluator? Do you develop offers?

❑ Would this case require two mediators?

❑ Will you help me understand my rights?

❑ Would you let me agree to a solution that you think is unfair?

❑ Should I have my own attorney present in this process? What role will the attorney play?

❑ What are the costs for a mediator? What happens if we don't reach a settlement? Could the case cost more than if we went to court? Who will handle logistics and costs?

❑ How likely do you think this case could be settled out of court?

❑ Do you meet with the parties individually at first or is it a joint session?

❑ How much background information will you gather about this case? If you aren't familiar with the subject will you research and learn about it? Will you talk to experts?

❑ How much experience do you have mediating? What are your strongest skills as a negotiator? Mediator?

❑ Are you certified? What did the certification process entail?

❑ What is your success rate for reaching settlements?

❏ How aware are you of your own biases, programming, and values?

❏ What understanding do you have of any cultural or other differences that may affect this case?

❏ Do you provide for special needs—interpreters, signers, handicap access?

❏ Have you handled cases like this before?

❏ What problems are likely to arise?

❏ How long could this process last?

❏ Are there outside people we should include in the process? Can I bring in witnesses or experts?

❏ Who will be responsible for preparing meeting summaries and other reports?

❏ Who drafts agreements? Do you and the parties have input into the wording of the agreement?

Ask Yourself During Mediation

❏ Does the mediator seem logical? Understanding? A good communicator?

❏ Does she listen well? Is she hearing me?

❏ Is the mediator acting as a neutral?

❏ Does the mediator continue to define and clarify the issues?

❏ Does she seem to have a good understanding of all the issues, interests, and needs in this case? Does she have all the information she needs?

❏ Do I understand the process, procedures, and language?

❏ Am I being open to negotiating an outcome?

❏ If there is a proposal on the table, what do I like and not like about the solution? What needs will and won't be met by this proposal? If I don't like the entire solution, which parts do I like and want? Can I be happy with this solution?

❏ Am I committed to following through on the agreement?

DON'T FORGET

❑ Call your local bar association for alternative dispute resolution resources.

❑ Call or write the National Institute for Dispute Resolution, 1726 M Street N.W., Suite 500, Washington, DC 20036-4502, 202-466-4764.

❑ For current information about the field of dispute resolution and available resources, call the Society of Professionals in Dispute Resolution, 202-833-2188.

❑ Call your local chapter of the American Arbitration Association or the national chapter for educational information (212-484-3266).

❑ Identify community mediation programs by calling your city or county.

❑ Get recommendations and references before hiring a mediator.

❑ Make sure you understand the process and language that is used. If you are at all confused, ask for clarification.

❑ If you are unhappy with a particular mediator, discontinue the process and request another mediator.

❑ Anticipate potential conflicts and write dispute resolution procedures into contracts.

Selecting an Insurance Agent

Jim and Bev decided to purchase a second-to-die life insurance policy to provide money for their heirs. Their insurance agent told them, based on the company's thirty-year history of returns on investments, that they would have to pay the premium for ten years and then the policy would be paid off. Jim and Bev faithfully paid this premium for ten years when they were informed by their insurance company that due to lower-than-average returns on the company's investments, they would have to continue to pay their premium for another three years — money they hadn't planned on spending. *Lessons learned*: Check with a few agents for insurance and to gain a more thorough understanding of specific transactions. Look closely at the history to see how they arrive at investment return statistics and whether this history shows a pattern for the future. Question the agent about different scenarios and understand what is a sure thing. Read all the fine print.

Insurance agents are either independent and buy products from several different companies or they work for a specific company and offer that company's insurance products. The most important factor when choosing an agent is to select a person you trust. If you don't have any referrals, call a reputable company.

Ask Yourself

❑ What type of insurance do I need—business, automobile, life, homeowner, medical, mortgage, property and casualty, liability, errors and omissions or professional liability, workmen's compensation, disability?

❑ How complex are my needs?

❑ Do I need an agent with extensive training such as a chartered property/casualty underwriter or chartered life underwriter?

❑ Do I want an independent agent or do I want to buy from an agent that represents a well-known company? An agent of a less well-known company?

❑ What kind of service will I be satisfied with?

Ask the Agent

❑ How long have you been in business? At least four or five years?

❑ Are you the owner of the company?

❑ Do you represent more than one company?

❑ Do you carry professional errors and omission insurance for yourself?

❑ How long has your agency been licensed with this insurance company?

❑ How long has this company been in business?

❑ What is this insurance company's rating? Is the company well capitalized? What happens if they can't make payments? Does the state guarantee claim payments? What is the cap?

❑ How accessible are you?

❑ Do you have someone in the office during working hours that can answer my questions?

❑ How often do you evaluate my needs?

❑ Are my policies automatically renewed each year?

❑ Do you check with me first?

❑ Do you check to see if the insuring company still offers the best deal for me?

❑ Will I be notified if you leave the agency? Who will notify me and when? Who will handle my policies if you leave?

❑ How do you keep current on changes that might affect my policies?

❑ What kind of insurance best meets my needs?

❑ Why is what you are offering the best policy for me?

❑ What do I do if my needs or circumstances change?

❑ What kinds of discounts are available on these policies (such as home security systems, smoke alarms, children on honor roll, no smoking, age)? Do I get reduced rates if I purchase more than one insurance policy from you?

❑ Am I covered for natural disasters such as earthquakes or hurricanes?

❑ Who handles claims? How quickly are they handled? Do I have to get several bids? Do I have to pay initially and then get reimbursed or do you pay directly?

❑ If I make a claim will my premiums increase? What are the increased charges?

❑ If you work directly for an insurer and I make a claim, whose interests are you most concerned with?

DON'T FORGET

❑ Get advice from accountants, attorneys, and financial planners about your insurance needs.

❑ Ask someone you trust to recommend an agent.

❑ Ask for the company's *A.M. Best* rating. This book is an industry standard that rates insurance companies on customer service issues such as how quickly they pay claims and how solid the company is.

❑ Ask what information you need to bring to a meeting discussing your insurance needs.

❑ Take note of your impressions. When you call the agency are you treated courteously and your calls returned promptly? Does the office seem well organized? Does the agent have a neat appearance?

❑ Don't buy on the first appointment unless you have thoroughly researched prices.

❑ Shop around for prices. If prices are different, understand why.

❑ Trust your instincts and comfort level with the person. If an agent tries to sell you a product before understanding your needs, don't use that agent.

Selecting a Bank

When my son moved back to Minneapolis he asked me what bank he should use. I suggested he call around. I wrote a list of questions for him to ask each institution. I looked through the abundance of promotional literature he received and discovered that my bank is offering computerized banking. I also found out that I could get a better deal on my checking account at two other banks. *Lessons learned*: Continually reassess your banking options. Changes in the banking industry, such as mergers and new computerized banking options, mean you must seek out information periodically to keep current. Many options can make choosing more difficult.

Ask As You Select General Banking Services

❑ Are you a full-service bank? Do you have checking accounts? Savings accounts? Retirement accounts? Financial planning? Mortgages? Other loans?

❑ Do you offer overdraft protection on checking and savings accounts? Is there a fee for either of these?

❑ Do you have home banking?

❑ Do you have a notary service at the bank? What is the fee?

❑ Do you provide free traveler's checks? Money orders? Cashier's checks? How do I qualify to receive these free? Is there a maximum number I can have free? If these services are not free, what are the fees for each?

❑ Do you have home equity loans? Are they fixed or variable rates? What are the rates? How quickly are applications processed?

❑ Do you offer student loans? At what interest rate? What is the repayment schedule? How quickly are student loans processed? Are there special requirements to obtain a student loan?

❑ Is there a fee for financial planning or setting up retirement accounts? What determines how you invest the money? Can you buy mutual funds, stocks, and annuities? Are you limited as to which products you can buy? What are those limitations?

❑ How much commission do you charge?

❑ Who do I work with? What are their qualifications?

❑ Can I get one monthly statement that consolidates all my accounts?

❑ Can I do telephone transfers between accounts? Is there a fee for this? Are there limitations on the number of transfers I can do by phone per month? Is there a maximum number of transfers I can do in a month?

❑ Can I automatically have a specified amount of money transferred from one account to another on a regular basis?

❑ Is there a fee for teller service?

❑ Does your bank issue credit cards? What is the interest rate? Is this an introductory offer and will it go up after a few months? How much?

❑ Can I pay bills by phone? Is there a fee?

❑ Are there types of accounts to consider that offer me discounts on loans or special rates on certificates of deposit?

❏ Can I get information about my account twenty-four hours a day? Is there a fee for using your automated bank-by-phone system to find out information about my account?

❏ Do you offer a revolving line of credit? What is the interest rate on the revolving line compared to a home equity loan or other type of loan?

❏ If I have a mortgage or loan at your bank can I have free checking? Other services for free or at a reduced rate?

❏ If I have checking and savings accounts at your bank, will it be easier to qualify for loans? What about business loans?

❏ Where are your branch offices? Do you have any branches in grocery stores or other places that I may frequent?

❏ What are your hours? Are you open on the weekends?

❏ Is there a fee for a monthly statement?

❏ Will you help balance my account if I need help? Is there a fee for this service?

❏ Do I pay more for a business checking or a business savings account?

❏ Do you have safe deposit facilities? Is there a fee?

❏ If you make an error do you pay me inconvenience money?

❏ Can I have money directly deposited to my accounts? What procedures do I need to follow?

❏ Do you have senior accounts that offer special services? What is the minimum age? What are the services, fees, and benefits?

❏ If any of the fees I pay or interest I receive is changed, do you inform me?

❏ Do you have facilities or services designed to accommodate my needs if I have a physical impairment?

❏ Do you have any clubs with benefits at your bank? How do I qualify? What are the benefits?

❏ Do you provide or sell my name to other companies? Can I sign a paper restricting your use of my name?

❑ What is your involvement in this community? Do you sponsor any community programs? What is your record of giving loans to minorities and women?

Ask About Banking by Computer

❑ Do you have computerized checking accounts?

❑ What software do you use? Can it work on my computer?

❑ Is there a fee to put it on my computer?

❑ Is there a monthly fee?

❑ Do I need a separate phone line?

❑ If a person or organization wants a check instead of electronic transfer do you send a check? If yes, is there an additional fee that I must pay?

❑ Will other people have access to my account? Do you have a computer security system to prevent people illegally accessing my accounts?

❑ Can I access customer service through the computer? How long does it take to get an answer? Will customer service be contacting me on the computer? Is there a fee for this?

❑ Do I still receive a monthly statement?

❑ Do I still have the option to write a paper check? How is it handled if I write a paper check?

❑ Are there any additional services that come with computerized banking? What are they?

❑ Can I tell you what day of the month to issue transfers to pay my bills or is my account debited immediately?

❑ Do you have an 800 number for computer customers?

Ask About Checking Accounts

❑ Do you have interest-bearing checking accounts? Is the interest variable or constant? If variable, how is it determined? How much is it likely to fluctuate? When and how is it compounded? Can you change the amount of interest without informing me?

❑ Is there a minimum amount of money I need to keep in the account? If so, what is the charge if I go below this amount? Will I collect interest on the minimum balance I leave in?

❑ Does my minimum balance need to be in my checking account or can it be combined with other savings plans I have?

❑ What other checking options are there? If I write few checks is it better to pay per check? What is the fee?

❑ Is it possible to switch types of accounts after opening one? Is there a charge?

❑ Do you have ready reserve checking accounts where loan money is available? What does it cost? What interest rate do you charge on the loan? What is the maximum loan that is available to me? What determines the amount? Do I have to pay anything for you to determine the loan amount? If my situation changes for the better can the loan amount I qualify for be changed? Will there be any fees related to changing?

❑ When I open an account with you will I receive free checks? How many? What is the reordering fee? Do I have my choice of checks? Can I get canceled checks with my monthly statement? Is there a fee for them? Are there other options?

❑ Is there a fee for depositing foreign checks?

❑ How soon can I write checks on money I deposit?

❑ How soon are deposits credited to my account? Does the time vary on weekends?

❑ What is the fee for stop payments on checks?

Ask About Savings Accounts

❑ What kinds of savings accounts and savings certificates are available?

❑ Is there a minimum amount required to open the account?

❑ What are the interest rates?

❑ Do I have to maintain a minimum daily balance?

❑ Do I need a passbook?

❑ Do I get a monthly statement of my savings account?

❑ How often is interest posted?

❑ Is there a minimum time the money needs to stay in the account before I use it? Is there a penalty if I withdraw it early? What determines that amount?

❑ Do I get unlimited withdrawals from my savings account if I withdraw in person? Are there fees for doing this?

❑ Do you have special savings accounts for children? What are the benefits of these accounts?

Ask About Cash Cards

❑ Do I automatically receive a cash card when I open an account?

❑ Is there any fee for the card?

❑ Is there a fee for withdrawing cash? Is the fee greater out of state or out of the country?

❑ Is there a maximum number of times I can use the card per day or per month without being charged? What is the per-use fee thereafter?

❑ Is there a maximum amount of money I can withdraw daily using my card? Can I extend the limit? How do I do that?

❑ Can I use the card to deposit money? Can I deposit money into both my savings and checking accounts with the card? How long does it take to post the deposit? Am I given credit for the deposit on my receipt before the bank actually posts it? How soon can I withdraw on the deposit?

❑ Can I use the card to withdraw from both my savings and checking? Do they have different limits? If I try to take money out of one account and it isn't available will it automatically withdraw the money from the other account?

❑ How quickly are withdrawals posted to my account?

❑ Can the card be used like a credit card and will funds be deducted from my account for purchases (a debit system)? Can I use it anywhere in the world?

❑ If I use the card for other purchases will it affect the amount of cash I can withdraw in a single day?

❑ Do I have overdraft privileges on the card?

❑ If I lose my cash card is there a replacement fee? How long does it take to get a card reissued? Do I have to come into a branch office to set up a new security number?

❑ Is there a fee if I want to obtain my account balance from a cash machine?

❑ If I lose my card, what is my liability?

❑ If I use my cash card as a debit card, do I have any recourse if I have a dispute with a merchant?

❑ How is it handled if the bank makes an error in paying my accounts?

❑ Should I keep receipts from purchases with this card?

Ask About Authorized Payment Deductions

❑ Is there a fee for authorized payment deductions?

❑ Is there a fee for stop payments on authorized payments? How much?

❑ What if a company withdraws more than I authorize them to?

❑ What happens if I don't have enough money in my checking account to cover automatic deductions? Will you still pay it? Do I have to pay a fee if you pay it? Would you notify me? When? How?

DON'T FORGET

❑ Be sure to make service-by-service comparisons to see which bank best meets your needs.

❑ If you hear of a new bank service, call and ask if your bank is offering this service.

❑ Continually check to see if there are better rates for you. As your circumstances change, you may want to change or add services (for example, some banks have special rates for people over 50 or 55).

Selecting an Accountant or Tax Service

David, an independent consultant, hired a CPA firm to prepare his income tax return. His two children each made a minimal amount of money at part-time summer jobs. He asked the accountant to prepare their returns also. David was billed three hundred dollars for each form—almost as much as each child earned. He learned an expensive lesson and the next year, he found a tax service that charged thirty-five dollars per form— a much more reasonable alternative. *Lessons learned*: Ask for a price first. Explore your options. Decide how much knowledge a person needs to have to do your work. A firm that does some of your work may not be appropriate to do all of your work.

Ask Yourself

❑ What are my needs—tax preparation, bookkeeping and accounting services, financial statements, financial planning, retirement and estate planning, business advice?

❑ Do I need tax help? Bookkeeping/accounting services? Financial statements? Financial planning? Retirement planning Estate planning? Business advice?

❑ Do I want to get all my needs met in one place?

❑ Do I need an accountant?

❑ What are my options? Do I understand the differences between certified public accountants (CPA), licensed public accountants (LPA), enrolled agents (EA), certified financial planners (CFP), and tax services?

❑ Can or should I bid out the services I'll need?

Ask the Accountant or Tax Service

❑ Do you charge for an initial interview?

❑ What is your expertise?

❑ What is your experience? How long have you been preparing taxes? What is your training?

❑ How familiar are you with my type of business? How much experience do you have working with my type of business?

❑ How do you keep your clients informed of changes in laws and procedures?

❑ How do you keep current on new laws and rules? How much continuing education do you have each year?

❑ Do you provide year-round services?

❑ Can I expect you to deliver on time?

❑ Has your firm had a quality review by a CPA outside your firm? Can I see your letter of comments?

❑ What do you do when you get in over your head on a technical question?

❑ What are your philosophies regarding IRS regulations? Do you consider yourself conservative, moderate, or aggressive?

❑ What do I need to do to maximize the accuracy and effectiveness of our relationship?

❑ Can you use the records prepared with my software?

❑ What type of management reports do you plan on providing? Will these reports be tailored to my business needs?

❑ Who else in the firm will be working on my account? Will the same people be continually working with the account? What is their experience? Can I meet them?

❑ For references, may I call a couple of your clients or will you have them call me?

❑ Do you stand by your work? If the IRS levies a fine because my returns are wrong, do you assume this cost?

❑ If any of the work is challenged, will you respond and attend hearings if necessary? Do I need to be present?

❑ How much do you charge? If you charge hourly, what time increments do you use? If others are working on my account do they charge a different rate? Use a different increment?

❑ Do I need to give you a retainer?

❑ Is there a minimum fee for tax returns or other work?

❑ Are there other fees in addition to your time such as forms, photocopying, phone calls, travel time?

DON'T FORGET

❑ Get referrals from friends and people in similar businesses.

❑ Interview several possibilities. You need to feel comfortable with the person or firm you hire.

❑ Consider bidding out work.

❑ Contact your state society of certified public accountants, state association of public accountants, or the state board of accountancy for referrals and helpful resources.

Selecting a
Financial Planner
or Broker

Harriet lost a great deal of money on a highly rated government institutional portfolio. Her broker said it was as safe as the U.S. government. She was told the portfolio comprised secure investments only and would remain that way. In fact, over time the portfolio's profile changed. Some of the fund's money was invested in derivatives which are contracts that give someone the right to buy a good or service at a specified price at some future date. This is speculative investing and earning a profit hinges on the portfolio manager's ability to predict an increase on this good or service in the future.

The first prospectus that Harriet saw—the one that influenced her purchasing decisions—did not say the portfolio contained derivatives. However, these were mentioned in later prospectuses. For a few years, Harriet earned a high rate of return and then the value of the portfolio dropped precipitously. She then learned how risky her "secure" investment had been. As in other transactions it is best to select a planner or broker that is referred by satisfied customers who you trust and whose priorities you understand. Advisers do not have crystal balls and there is no guarantee that their recommendations will be fruitful. You need to be actively involved in understanding your options and in making decisions.

Lessons learned: Seek brokers that research even their own company's products. Advisers are usually commissioned sales people who have their own agenda. All investments involve risk. Investments might not turn out the way you expect. Read all your investment literature. Save all your paperwork. Because a person is nice doesn't mean that he is thorough, trustworthy, or outstanding. Finally, financial advisers can be wrong. There are no regulations about who can call themselves a financial planner so choose carefully.

Ask Yourself

❏ Do I have a thorough understanding of my financial situation, needs, and goals?

❏ What is most important to me as I make investments—the types of businesses I want to invest in, return on my money, dividends, steady income, predictable earnings?

❏ How comfortable am I with risk? How great a risk do I want to take and with what percentage of my money?

❏ What kind of advice and assistance do I want—retirement planning, taxes, income-producing investments?

❏ Do I want to make my own decisions and use someone to buy for me? Do I want help with all my decisions and purchases? Or do I want some of both? Do I want to consider a discount broker for stock purchases?

❏ Do I want to use one person who has a wide range of knowledge and products or a number of specialists who work in specific areas?

Ask an Adviser

❏ What do you specialize in? What are your interests?

❏ Do you watch particular markets?

❏ What is your investment philosophy?

❑ Do you have firsthand experience or do you turn to a company adviser?

❑ How familiar are you with the people and companies selling these products? What percentage of your clientele is involved in these type of investments?

❑ If I need access to my money, how would you recommend it be invested?

❑ If I need a fixed income, how would you recommend it be invested?

❑ If I am looking for long-term investments, what would you recommend?

❑ What is the risk factor in each of your recommendations?

❑ What are your training, experience, and track record?

❑ How long has your firm been in business?

❑ How often do you meet with me to reassess my goals, portfolio, and needs?

❑ Will you send me monthly status reports?

❑ Is your company full service? Will you research a product I am interested in? Is there a fee?

❑ How are you compensated?

❑ If you work on commission, will you ever recommend products to me even if you won't get any commission but that may be of interest or benefit to me?

❑ Is your commission based on the number of shares I buy or sell or on the value of the transaction?

❑ Are there minimum and maximum fees? Are there additional fees I might need to pay? Expenses incurred? Are there rebates if I have frequent transactions or if commissions exceed a specified amount?

❑ If you charge an hourly rate, what is your fee? What is the estimated time it would take you to evaluate my needs? What would be the estimated ongoing amount of time you'll need to manage my account?

❑ If you charge fees and work on commission, are the fees applied to your commission if I purchase your suggestions?

❑ Are you limited to selling your company's products?

❑ Will you tell me when you are selling from your company's inventory and I may be paying a markup? (This is required by law.)

❑ Do you have certain products that your company encourages you to sell at specific times? Do you research those products or take someone else's word for them? Do you have quotas to meet?

❑ How objective can you be in evaluating my needs?

❑ How am I to know if what you are suggesting is in my best interest, your best interest, or your organization's best interest?

❑ What is the range of products your organization handles — insurance, stocks, mutual funds, bonds, money markets?

❑ Do you discount your rates for stock and bond transactions? Under what circumstances?

❑ Do you offer automated trading services?

❑ How do you keep track of my requests?

❑ Is there an arbitration agreement in any of the contracts I need to sign?

DON'T FORGET

❑ Make sure that financial consultants ask about, understand, and are focused on your needs.

❑ Get several referrals from friends and colleagues. Interview them all at least by phone.

❑ Get references.

❑ Take classes offered in your community or by various firms.

❑ Obtain background information on the broker and the firm by contacting the National Association of Securities Dealers, 1735 K Street, Washington, DC 20006 or call 1-800-284-9999.

❑ Don't give your adviser permission to trade your account at her discretion.

❑ Don't invest in something you don't understand.

❑ Be aware of the downside risks of all your investments.

❑ Fees vary by transaction and brokers. If you are concerned about fees, shop around before making each transaction.

❑ Read books and articles about investments. For more in-depth information read *Investors Rights Handbook* by Larry D. Soderquist.

❑ Check to see if your planner belongs to the International Association of Financial Planners. Ask the IAFP for a list of qualified planners in your area and for helpful brochures or publications (1–800–345–IAFP).

❑ If you are looking for a discount broker there are several sources, including *The Discount Financial Directory* published annually by Mercer, Inc.

❑ Don't stay with a broker if his behavior makes you uncomfortable. If you are being pressured or told you have to buy fast or it will be sold out, that's a red flag. Be skeptical of anyone who says any investment is a sure thing.

❑ Might I like to work with people who use alternative techniques such as art, dance, or music therapy to uncover issues?

❑ Do I feel comfortable with this person?

Ask the Therapist

❑ What are your educational background, training, and experience?

❑ Are you licensed in the state?

❑ How do you keep current on your field and the latest research? Do you continue to take classes? What do you do for professional development?

❑ Have you gone through therapy yourself?

❑ Are you aware of your biases and how they may affect my therapy?

❑ How do you decide if I need more than you can do for me?

❑ Do you work with psychiatrists (if a therapist) or therapists (if a psychiatrist)?

❑ Do you have a specialty?

❑ Do you incorporate different theories or use just one theory? If one, which one and what are the basic premises behind the theory?

❑ What is your approach? Do you believe in modifying behavior? Looking for root causes? Hypnosis?

❑ Have you dealt with other cases similar to mine? What kinds of changes have your clients made?

❑ What are your expectations of me?

❑ Will you need to meet other family members?

❑ Do you counsel more than one family member at the same time? If you do, how do you keep issues and relationships separate?

❑ How many sessions do you expect me to need?

❑ Do you support me through change efforts? Might you refer me to groups that will be helpful in my change effort?

❑ Will you share this information with anyone?

❑ Do you discuss cases with colleagues to get other opinions?

❑ Are you licensed to prescribe medication? How do I know if I need medication?

❑ Do you belong to professional organizations?

❑ Can you be reached in case of an emergency?

❑ Do you have a colleague who helps your patients when you're away and unavailable?

❑ Who else takes your calls? What are her qualifications?

❑ What are your fees?

❑ Are you covered by insurance?

❑ Do you submit directly for insurance or do I prepay and get reimbursed?

❑ What methods of payment do you accept?

❑ Is there a limit as to how many sessions or how much time insurance will cover?

❑ Do you have group sessions that may be less expensive?

DON'T FORGET

❑ Get referrals from friends, family, doctors, people who have had good experiences with therapists. Ask them why they liked their therapist and what their priorities are in selecting one.

❑ Interview two or three therapists on the phone and select one that you like.

❑ Meet with the therapist and see how you get along. Chemistry is important.

❑ Have a clear contract with the therapist about what you want to work on, the rules, and boundaries.

❑ Notice if the therapist practices what was described in your phone interview.

❏ Make sure the therapist treats you respectfully. You should not be labeled, blamed, shamed, or put down. There is no singular way for everybody.

❏ Check credentials with professional organizations.

❏ Watch for any sexual overtures. The counselor should not be using herself to help you overcome sexual issues.

Using a Library

One day a house guest came with me to use the library while I consulted with librarians. When I finished, I discovered she had not located the information she needed. She had asked someone for help. He pointed her to a computer terminal but didn't help her use it to locate the material she needed. She couldn't figure out how to use it on her own so she gave up. As it turned out, she had asked an aide for assistance, not a librarian. The aide didn't direct her to a librarian for further assistance.

In his book *Powershift* Alvin Toffler talks about knowledge as the principal power of the twenty-first century. Today, it is more important than ever to know where to go to get the information you need and to assess the accuracy of that information. Libraries are becoming increasingly important resources. Some have extensive and elaborate computer systems, larger collections of specific information, video and audio tapes, art rentals, recording and editing equipment, and more.

Lessons learned: You need to make sure you find the people who are trained to help you. You need to clearly ask for what you need. If systems designed to help library users locate material do not have easy-to-follow instructions, ask for help.

Ask Yourself

❑ What information do I really need?

❑ How am I going to use this information?

❑ What is the best place to get it? Might there be an association or organization I can get the information from directly, or do I need a library?

❑ What format do I want the information in — text, lists, abstracts, statistics, quotations, reviews?

❑ Do I need the most current information?

❑ Do I need to refer to books that might be in a historical collection?

❑ Do I need to physically go to a library, can I call a reference desk for the information, or can I access the library's resources through my computer?

❑ Do I have access to on-line computer references that will be sufficient?

Ask About the Library

❑ How do you have your resource information stored — format journals, books, videos, compact discs, or CD ROM?

❑ What materials are available for me to check out — records, audiotapes, art, books, computer programs, games, videos?

❑ What kind of equipment do you have for patrons to use — computers, copy machines, film editing equipment, anything else?

❑ Do you have viewing rooms if I want to watch a video?

❑ Are there charges for various services? What are they?

❑ Can I access your catalog from my computer terminal? If yes, what is the process?

❑ Can you fax information to me?

❑ Do you specialize in certain collections?

❑ Do you offer tours of the library? Do you have sessions to acquaint people with information-gathering resources and techniques?

❑ Do you have any private areas that are particularly quiet?

❑ Are there libraries that have more of what I want?

❑ Do you have a list of area libraries?

❑ Can you get what I want from other systems if you don't have it? How long will it take? Is there any fee for this service?

❑ If what I want is out, do you keep a waiting list?

❑ If I have any specific requests for you to stock materials that you don't have, whom can I talk to?

❑ What are your hours?

❑ Are there rental fees for specific collections such as videos, art, or other resources?

❑ What kinds of activities do you have for children? Is there a regular schedule?

❑ Do parents need to be present during these activities?

❑ Do you have programs for adults?

❑ Do you have rooms available for community or business groups to use? Is there a charge for using them?

❑ Do you know of experts who can address groups on particular subjects?

❑ Do you need volunteers in the library? What are your volunteer opportunities?

❑ Should I reshelve the materials I use or should I put them somewhere else?

❑ Can I call ahead and ask about the library's resources on a specific topic? Will a librarian check to make sure the facility has the materials I need before I go there?

❑ Is there a certain time that would be better for me to come in to get specific help?

❑ Are there particular librarians who are more familiar with my topic? When is the best time to talk with them?

❏ Could you please show me how to use your computer system to locate what I need? What key words would you suggest I use to find the information?

DON'T FORGET

❏ Tell the librarian what kind of information you need and why you need it rather than asking for specific materials. This way the librarian may guide you toward some additional, helpful resources.

❏ Consider asking different librarians for ideas.

❏ If a library doesn't carry what you want, talk to the acquisitions librarian.

❏ If you have trouble locating information or want to have someone else find, evaluate, or synthesize information, consider asking a librarian for the name of an information broker. This is someone who, for a fee, specializes in locating and gathering information. Otherwise call the Association of Independent Information Professionals (212–779–1855) or check your yellow pages.

❏ Be appreciative.